A HOUSE FOR MR MISRA

A HOUSE FOR MR MISRA

Jaishree Misra

Westland Publications Ltd

61, II Floor, Silverline Building, Alapakkam Main Road,
Maduravoyal, Chennai 600095

93, I Floor, Sham Lal Road, Daryaganj, New Delhi 110002

First published by Westland Publications Ltd 2017

10 9 8 7 6 5 4 3 2 1

ISBN: 9789386850485

Typeset in Scala by SÜRYA, New Delhi

Printed at Thomson Press (India) Ltd.

For Ranjana and Bharat,
without whose help there would be no house
and certainly a much longer book.

1

WHATEVER CAME OVER ME? AGREEING TO MOVE TO the other side of the world was mad enough, but to build a house slap bang against one of the widest, wildest oceans in the world? And I do mean 'slap bang'. The plot of land we bought lay so close to the sea, the waves lashed with terrifying ferocity against our brand-new back gate during the first rainy season and nearly washed it away. I watched the fisherman who lived next door use a stout piece of rope to tie our gate to a nearby palm tree. Then I looked at the unruly waves surging up at the very edge of our plot with the strangest feeling of standing on the prow of a storm-tossed ship, all hands on deck, shiver me timbers, etc. And no, I did not adopt the Kate Winslet-arms-out-billowing stance even though thoughts of the *Titanic* weren't far from my mind.

The sea abutting our newly purchased piece of land was the Indian Ocean which, during the monsoon season, heaves and bucks against a rapidly retreating shoreline on the southern Indian peninsula, its waves growing in menacing proportions to crash onto what's left by then of beach and the row of tiny fishermen's houses that cling in terror to the shore. The boom-boom sound was like cannon fire in a never-ending war. And we were about to enter that war zone. Willingly, voluntarily, with nobody holding a gun to our heads.

I mean, we lived in London. *London*. Amiable, multicultural, multilingual London with its trundling red buses and elegant town-houses lounging graciously around leafy squares and, oh, all those theatres and museums packed to the rafters with history and culture and all manner of art. Apart from the endearing fact that London sat on terra firma with no ocean anywhere in its vicinity, wasn't it where everyone else wanted to be? Certainly everyone I knew in India was trying to get to London, paying a large portion of an average monthly salary just to get a tourist visa, never mind the flights and exorbitant hotels. I wasn't oblivious to the envious looks when I mentioned where I lived.

Just so you get the full picture, we had the dinkiest house near the south bank of the Thames, a pretty little period property in Borough, ten minutes from a famed 250-year-old food market where, if the fancy struck me, I could buy oysters on gleaming hillocks of crushed ice, jewel-red acai berry juice bursting with antioxidants, and breakfast granola in eight different flavours. Not to forget those chunky salted caramel brownies at the fabulous Cadbury-purple fronted Konditor & Cook, the best cake shop in town in my well-researched opinion. In recent times Borough market had joined the ranks of London's top attractions, and I had started to see coachloads of tourists disembarking from buses marked 'Sussex Tours' or 'Kentish Travels', all armed with enormous shopping bags, faces gleaming with greed.

(NB. In a heart-twistingly sad way I could see why those terrorists in the UK's recent summer night attack chose Borough Market. They could not have found a jollier, more lively place to wreak havoc, and the victims, caught so tragically on a Saturday night out, were, without exception, young and attractive and fun-loving.)

There's more on our London home. From its front door, the Tate Modern, arguably the world's greatest modern art gallery, was a twelve-minute walk (*and* they'd started building the extension the year we left), the South Bank Centre with its numerous stages and the buzzing BFI theatre next door were a leisurely fifteen-minute stroll and the West End and Covent Garden (all those cheeky street performances and Parisian-style cafés where waiters with French accents served up *joli colore* macarons on *bijou plats*) was less than half an hour away, a pleasurable jaunt up and over Waterloo Bridge where tourist boats tooted as they passed beneath and their happy, camera-wielding passengers waved to bridge-walkers like me, excited beyond belief at our combined luck to actually be traipsing around this rollicking city.

Oh, and did I say I had a job that was the envy of all my friends? I was an Examiner at the British Board of Film Classification (BBFC) where, as a friend once asked rather plaintively, 'They actually *pay* you to watch films!?' My office in Soho was a forty-minute walk from my front door, a daily constitutional that provided as much entertainment as exercise. It had become happy custom to reward myself as I neared work with a glass of freshly squeezed organic juice from a street vendor on Earlham Road although, had I preferred coffee, I could have nipped into Starbucks around the corner or Pret or Costa or Eat, where, once a week, I treated myself to a tuna cheese melt at lunch. In fact, if at this point I decided to divert this book into a food and beverage catalogue of Soho, I could instantly go off on an endless and tortuous tangent.

Oh yes, Soho was seductive. And not only in its historic way, though elements of the old red light district still existed—mostly in the form of sex shops where one could browse for anything from vibrators to giant strap-on dildos, the very sight of which could make your eyes water.

Every Thursday, Mr M arrived as I was finishing work to join me at the BBFC's staff-screening of the latest big release and, having been indulged thus, we piled on yet another favourite treat by strolling down to Chinatown for a platter of Singapore Noodles and barbequed pork on rice served with the most garlicky gailan tossed up anywhere in the Western hemisphere.

And yet, YET, there we were kicking beach-sand into the face of all that bounty to stand at the edge of a small plot on the outskirts of a muggy, ragged pre-monsoonal Trivandrum, looking at a broken-down yellow house with the weirdest idea that it could become our future home.

The house belonged to a fish broker who could not seem to believe his luck at having buyers like us fall idiotically into his lap. With dollar signs pulsing in his eyes, he had started off with a flabbergasting 'NRI' price, and we had already spent a couple of hours, the hot sun beating down on our heads, trying to bring the rate down to a more reasonable level.

True, the plot was right next to a sandy beach, albeit strewn at the moment with dried seaweed and all manner of human detritus from solitary rubber chappals to empty Sprite bottles. And the Laccadive sea (the romantic name dredged up by Mr M when I paled at the sound of 'Indian Ocean') lay sparkling less than fifty yards away. But this was Kerala. *Kerala*. The place I had run away from twenty years ago, fleeing an unsuccessful arranged marriage and a stubbornly conservative society. Besides, there were all kinds of regulations protecting India's coastline, which meant we would probably *never* be able to renovate the ruin we were buying and make it liveable. I say 'probably' even though much of the story that follows proves it to be indubitably the case. But more on that anon.

For now it looked alarmingly like we were on the verge of giving up our comfortable (if somewhat calorific) London life to live on the other side of the world in a hovel with a leaking roof and cracked concrete floors. So why was I not shrieking in protest, I hear you ask.

Contemplating such a shriek, I cast another disbelieving eye around my newly adopted environs, heart settling firmly into my feet. The overgrown compound was littered with what was surely ten years' supply of discarded plastic milk sachets, some of which were festooning an enormous cactus standing at the bottom of the garden like a comedy Christmas tree. Amidst the scrubby growth were a few impressive craggy anthills out of whose labyrinthine interiors armies emerged to march with great purpose into the house which clearly served as Ant Headquarters.

'There's an electricity connection,' Mr M exclaimed, latching on to the one identifiable plus point of the house. He gestured to a long black wire that looped through one window to attach itself precariously to the lamppost on the street outside.

'But no water connection,' I replied. 'Apparently the well services the needs of the household.'

We looked at the small rusty pump nestled next to a hole in the ground. A green rubber pipe snaked from one end of the pump, winding its way up to a small plastic tank on the roof. The 'well' had the barest wall around it—less than a foot in height—and I stood at a safe distance in order to peer in. My anxious face shimmered back at me from a brackish mirror.

'A child fell in there once,' a neighbour said, her head poking over a mossy wall.

'But his father jumped in and saved him,' the head next to hers clarified.

'The child was saved but, later, a cat fell in.'

'Ah yes, that one died in there.'

In the murky depths were what could have been a cat skeleton or a few floating bones. Certainly the oily black scum bore little resemblance to the stuff that emerged from my taps at home. I narrowed my gaze and peered again, wondering if we may indeed be striking it lucky by buying an oil well but, no, it really was just filthy water laced with the decomposing skeletons of small mammals or children. And they said London's water was undrinkable.

I dragged my gaze away as I realised that our presence had brought a sizeable crowd to the plot. Half the neighbourhood—mostly a fishing community—had by now assembled in the compound to 'help' in the negotiations. No one was on our side, from what I could see, so we were essentially taking on a small army. Or, as happens in Kerala, a minor union which, for those who know Kerala, is a lot more formidable than an army.

The house owner suddenly capitulated on the price. I thought it might have been because he'd spotted that look on my face which Mother described as 'her curdled milk face', but I soon gathered that someone had just reminded him the house wasn't in his name. It was another garbled story, rendered with dramatic flourish, the neighbours chipping in with background information like a Greek chorus. What I discovered very gradually was that the 'owner' had, in a fit of paternal love, legally passed the land on which the house stood to his adopted son. The son, having grown up and got married, had fallen in love with his wife but fallen out with his father and now barely saw him. Son had subsequently and cannily transferred ownership of the house to his wife to render it doubly difficult for the father to claim it back. The latter, however, fearing that his son would at some point stake his claim to live in the house, thereby rendering him homeless, had started court proceedings to do precisely that, i.e., get ownership of the house back.

So that turned out to be the other thing—we were not only buying a broken-down hovel in Kerala, we were buying one that was in legal dispute. In a country where legal disputes took an average of thirty-four years to resolve.

Nevertheless, Mr M was sure he wanted the house. To be fair, he had spent every India holiday these past six years combing Kerala's coastline for a plot to build his dream beach-house on. It had to be a piece of land with direct access to a road as well as a proper view of the sea, not offer mere glimpses of distant blue as was the case with the many plots we had been shown by property brokers. Okay, he hadn't combed *all* of Kerala's coastline, but he'd certainly traversed the stretch that started at Poovar beach and travelled north, past bays and lighthouses and unattractive conurbations, about 30 km, to palm-fringed Puthenthope. He'd once even made a half-hearted offer on a plot in Puthenthope but had backed out when he realised that, if he followed Corporation rules and built on the footprint of the existing house, he'd get no view at all of the sea, which was yards away at the wrong end of the plot, and instead be living right up against the busy road that connected Kazhakootam to Quilon.

This wasn't unusual: everyone in Kerala built houses like that as 'roadside' commanded a huge premium in real estate. Malayalis, other than fishermen, build houses on the beach only if they can afford no other place in town, almost always preferring to stay as safely away from the sea as they can. It is my belief that the typical Malayali brain has an overdeveloped fear/anxiety centre in the amygdala. Which is why, when presented with a decision as innocent as say, whether to buy an ice-cream cone, it's the worst-case scenario that I will *always* consider first (e.g., Hepatitis B, typhoid, gastroenteritis and sore throat, in roughly that order) until I finally succumb to temptation. Whether it is due to this curious communal psychological feature or not, the sea in Kerala is definitely respected and feared by most of its citizens. Unlike in Western countries, beaches aren't places of pleasure and relaxation to the typical Malayali. They are where the fishing communities work their trade and, because fishermen drink like ... well, like fish ... in the long days that stretch ahead of them once their dawn run is done, they sometime get into fights as drunken people often do. Stories of knifings and assaults are rife and the rest of Kerala's population prefers to stay as far away as possible from this explosive mix of natural and manmade disasters. On the rare occasion when they do visit the beach, it is to stand at a safe distance and watch a magnificent sunset or shoot a bit of breeze. Indeed, it is a rare Malayali man who, in making this annual excursion to the beach, will have chosen to exchange his customary trousers, half-sleeved shirt, socks and shoes for shorts and a tee-shirt. It's essential to always be in a state of readiness for flight, you see. Plus, one must always strive to look *decent*.

The women, on the other hand, are generally more game for the 'fight' option (and apparently more willing to dally with the occasional indecency too), so are often to be seen linking hands and raising saris to knee-height while running into the churning waves to the accompaniment of happy shrieks.

SO. Why was I—the Malayali in this marriage, who should have heeded her own fight-or-flight instinct—being corralled into this madcap venture, you may well ask. Was it the pioneering spirit of our ancient beach-combing ancestors that Michael Wood had informed me about on the telly? I wish I could say it was because that would be a story truly worth telling, filled with adventure and derring-do, in which amygdalae did not figure at all. The rather less glamorous truth was that Mr M and I were refugees of the Western recession. Ironically, the journey we had both made from East to West as young educational and economic migrants was now taking place in reverse. I have a theory that, if you live long enough, you will get to see everything that is currently sacrosanct being turned helplessly on its head, but this backflip had taken less than thirty years.

Mr M had left for the UK as an eighteen-year-old student to get a decent education and find a job. In India of the '80s, the prospects were bleak unless you had made it past the IIT entrance exams. In England, he had gone on (at terrible cost to his youth and libido, he'd often tried persuading me) to sit a number of exams that qualified him to become a member of the august Institute of the Chartered Accountants of England and Wales and his last job had been that of Finance Director of Eurostar. Yes, the company whose trains shuttle between glamorous destinations like Paris and London and Brussels. We had so many free passes in those years, there were times we travelled to Paris for lunch. On a whim. First Class. Cute little bottles of wine and tablets of Belgian chocolate wrapped in gold foil served with every meal. Somewhere along the way, Mr M had left that job to freelance as a consultant to Deloitte, now earning money at eye-popping hourly rates. But, a few years later, all that plenitude had suddenly come to nought when the recession blew like a transatlantic typhoon from America to hit British shores. Lucrative freelance work was the first to dry up and Mr M had spent a few months moping around the house, having unexpectedly become Chief Householder in charge of larder and laundry while I sat in a swank Soho office, being *paid* to watch films all day. However confident and however feminist, the switch from CFO to CH is a mortifying one for anyone and, dare I say it, for men in particular, who fail to spot the opportunities on offer, not least the time to sit around all day sipping coffee and finally reading all those unread books in our library. But that didn't suit Mr M's go-getting personality at all, and it was clear that he was not going to find a decent job in the current Western climate. Not for a long, long time were we likely to spot those green shoots of recovery our politicians promised us, like we were a nation of fools. Even my workplace—the stolid and reliable BBFC that had stood at Soho Square like a pillar of the British establishment for near on a hundred years—had started murmuring about laying off people because of diminishing film-submission levels and, in order to tempt staff to leave, announced a generous voluntary redundancy scheme. Much as I loved my job, this was an alluring prospect. Not merely being given a year's salary for zero work but also being able to leave an organisation where the spectre of redundancies was swiftly turning the atmosphere sour.

The writing was starting to form itself on the walls of our comfortable little house in Borough. Mr M needed to stop leafing mournfully through the FT week after week, searching for non-existent jobs. We could, after all, rent out the house in Borough for a tidy sum, seeing how close it was to the financial district. Our daughter—a young woman with special needs—was well settled in a care-home in Kent that was the safest and most stimulating environment we could have ever hoped to find for her and so she wasn't dependent on us anymore. Plus she could spend the long winter hols warming her bones with us in India. Our two mothers, both of whom were widows, would be delighted to have us nearby after all these years of rushed and unsatisfying annual holiday visits. And, if we were going to live in India, then why not consider Trivandrum where my mother lived? Our other option—Delhi, where we had both grown up—was now a polluted mess where one spent half of an average day stuck in traffic jams. The advent of the internet had made living in smaller towns a feasible prospect. In Kerala, Mr M could begin to work on his long-held dream of a house on the beach while I wrote a book or two ... I'd never seen a bigger smile on his face when I finally said yes.

2

ONCE THE PRICE HAD BEEN AGREED UPON, WE PAID the seller an advance and laid down three conditions.

1. The father would have to withdraw the court case.
2. The son would sign an agreement to give half of the sale proceedings to his father.
3. The father would use part of the advance to build a wall around the property which, at the moment, lay open to neighbouring plots, a nearby tourist walkway and the beach.

This last clause was included by my canny

uncle, who informed us that land ownership papers often bore little resemblance to actuality on the ground and, if there were going to be disputes over boundaries, it was for the seller to sort them out and not us.

Did I just say 'dispute'? For that is a very polite way to describe what we did witness when we went to Veli a couple of days later to have a look at the wall that was being built. In fact, we could hear the blood-curdling yelling even as we parked the car on a nearby empty plot and walked up to the house.

Seller's neighbour—a fisherman—had a hut that was cheek by jowl with Seller's house and he now cut a fearsome figure as he stood in his doorway, wearing a lungi and waving an old-fashioned *vettukatthi* in the air, shouting at the world in general with Seller's name making occasional appearances. The cutlass was not a throwback to some ancient piratical custom but merely the implement that is used locally to fell and crack open coconuts. Every household has one of these and sometimes they figure in newspaper reports of a gory murder somewhere or the other. Seeing it being waved about to the accompaniment of shouted insults therefore made for a rather terrifying sight.

These neighbours were a Hindu–Christian couple who had apparently always shared an uneasy relationship with Seller who was Muslim. Religious disharmony (not common in Kerala) probably had less to do with it than the fact that Seller was a middle-man and therefore not the most popular figure amongst the fisher folk. Most significantly, however, Seller had that morning tied the marking thread to build his wall right across the piece of land that was used by the neighbour to pull his boat up from the beach during the monsoons. By building the wall thus, he would effectively prevent his neighbour from accessing the path he had used for years to bring his boat to safety during the pre-monsoonal high-tides of May. In another bid to elongate his plot as much as he possibly could, Seller had stretched the thread all the way across to the tourist walkway. While it was entirely possible that he was indeed legal owner of all this land, we gathered through all the shouting (yes, a crowd had gathered again and looked, mysteriously, like a whole new set of faces) that this would effectively block off the route that was taken every year by the local church procession on St Sebastian's Day. So Neighbour and his wife and most of the good Christians who had gathered were naturally upset enough to call Seller's entire lineage into question. I knew the local Christian community was a powerful and wealthy lobby group—only a few days ago we had wandered into the newly-built Kochuveli church and found ourselves amazed by the lavish stretches of polished wood and marble and stained glass. Even the ceiling fans were so massive, they would have put jet engine propellers to shame. A worshipper told us, laughing, that the first time they were turned on, hymn books went flying while saris billowed shamelessly in the air.

Despite the collective shouting, I noticed nobody mentioned the Muslim–Christian angle, which was really rather admirable considering that, in most other parts of India, religion would have swiftly become the main point of contention in such an altercation. Kerala's record of communal harmony was holding strong even here, in presently strife-torn Veli.

Canny Uncle was with us on this occasion and so a summit was hastily held, right there in Seller's compound, with Uncle presiding in avuncular manner while empty milk sachets blew around our ankles in the breeze. It was agreed that Seller would leave enough room next to the walkway, with space both for the church procession as well as access for Neighbour's boat to be hauled up during the monsoon. What remained unspoken was that, while we would get a few feet less of compound, we would rather fortuitously make a saving on buying land we didn't really need. Plus, we wouldn't be in the bad books of every single Christian within a three-mile radius of where we lived. Veli was a predominantly Christian community, and we had saved ourselves from having about a hundred thousand new enemies in the neighbourhood as well as ensuring many peaceful St Sebastian's Days ahead. Having achieved this major feat, we took Canny Uncle to the Trivandrum Tennis Club to raise a few glasses in tribute to his canniness.

Our next visit to Veli was more dramatic and a great deal more sobering. The small wall had been built by now and Neighbour was satisfied enough with its position to even throw us a wave over it with no sign of the cutlass in his hand. However, a couple of hours later, we heard a different kind of shouting from the beach. This in itself wasn't unusual as we had already found Veli's seaside to be a noisy environment, what with the fishermen's hoots to announce a good catch and their chants of encouragement to each other when a boat was hauled in. Nevertheless, we climbed onto the walkway to have a look. From other people gathered nearby, we found that a man—an autorickshaw driver from a neighbouring locality—had gone missing. He had been paddling with four friends when they all decided to go out a little further for a swim, but on their return the group discovered that their headcount wasn't quite right. Of course, the sea isn't the sort of place one could send a search party into (nobody mentioned a coast-guard service at any rate), and so there was nothing anyone could do but wait with diminishing hope that the missing man would somehow struggle back to the shore. His family arrived in another autorickshaw and my heart went out to the two silently weeping women who sat next to where the man's clothes and slippers lay in a neat pile on the concrete walkway. The local fishermen, on the other hand, were muttering disapprovingly at the drunken antics of beach frolickers, and I gathered that such drownings were a regular affair.

'One every six months,' one of the neighbours stated matter-of-factly.

'Bloody drunks,' another woman said.

'When these men want to sneak away from their wives to drink, they come here to our beach.'

'And when they have too much to drink, they think they can take on the sea.'

'Bloody idiot drunks, making trouble for us,' the other woman repeated.

'Remember, the last time a man drowned here, it was Vijayan's boat that came back with the body.'

'They managed to find it in the sea?' I asked, incredulous.

'The body got entangled in their nets and so they just hauled it up and brought it back to the shore.'

'Losing their day's catch, of course. Idiot trouble-making drunks.'

I knew enough about Kerala's bibulous ways to understand what a massive problem alcoholism had become. Some surveys put Kerala alongside Andhra Pradesh as the biggest per capita consumer of alcohol in India. More specifically, the National Sample Survey Office had recently recorded the state's per capita consumption at 16 ml per week or 10.2 litres a year. Not a small figure, given that most women and children did not imbibe alcoholic beverages, which automatically trebled the amount the men were drinking. It was no surprise too that, while other states consumed more toddy and country liquor, Kerala's preference was for beer and the oddly named IMFL, an acronym for Indian Made Foreign Liquor. So, being a more prosperous state had only helped make it more finicky in its taste for alcohol. Concerned that this was now spilling over into drug use and domestic abuse, the

UDF government had, in 2014, made a ham-fisted attempt at prohibition, closing down bars across the state and allowing only five-star hotels to sell alcoholic beverages. Naturally, bar-owners and small hoteliers and resort-owners went up in arms, but TV images had shown great gatherings of women crowding the gates of Cliff House, where Chief Minister Oomen Chandy lived, to ... yes, to thank him for this favour. It was clearly a battle of the sexes. From the way things generally went in Kerala, I could not help seeing the sizzle of a giant damp squib marked 'Prohibition' lying ahead. Sure enough, I read recently that the LDF government had (presumably with great glee) overturned the UDF government's ruling to enable three- and four-star hotels to sell alcohol once again.

I cast another glance at the two women who were sitting on the Veli walkway, still weeping for the lost man. Was he a brother or a husband, who knew? And was he drunk, as the locals claimed, or was the sea reminding everyone of its ultimate power over us mere mortals?

It lay gleaming serenely today, swelling and subsiding in the distance, holding on to its mysteries. I wondered what sort of a neighbour this huge, unpredictable force would make. Mr M was an avid sea-swimmer, but the poor missing autorickshaw driver was proof that it really did make sense sometimes to listen to one's amygdala.

3

'THEY'RE DEMANDING HALF THE MONEY IN BLACK,' Mr M said. (This dialogue was, of course, taking place in those halcyon days before demonetisation.)

'Whaat!? But we don't have black money. We're law-abiding British citizens, remember?' When Mr M continued to look pleadingly at me, I added, 'And you're a member of the Institute of Chartered Accountants of England and Wales? Years and years of exams to get qualified? At the cost of your youth and libido?'

'Yes, yes, but it's not *us* doing anything illegal, it's them.'

'But we'll be kind of aiding and abetting,

wouldn't we? Besides, we don't *have* any black money.' I hoped I'd clinched the argument with that reminder.

'It's dead easy converting white money to black,' he replied, hesitating only a fraction.

'Is it?' I have never been very good with money in the first place and had not the vaguest notion of how changing its colour could be achieved. 'I mean, surely we'll be arrested if we get found out. Just tell them no. They'll have to take what we give them. Tell them it's *good* cash, hard earned, sweat of our brows, you labouring over spreadsheets and me watching Teletubbies and wrestling DVDs till I'm squint-eyed, etc. etc.'

Mr M's voice took on a wheedling tone. 'Well, the old man needs money—cash—if he is to pay his son and daughter-in-law off. Apparently they're actually talking to each other now. Think of it, we could be getting a family back together again.'

My Mr M didn't have the teeniest social

worker lurking within him but I ignored this convenient makeover. 'The daughter-in-law's the legal owner, isn't she? So shouldn't we be paying her and then her husband pays his father off?'

'Not sure that'll work, seeing that it's the father who is actually living in the house. And he won't budge if they don't pay him what he wants. We'll need to keep them all sweet. The bottom line is they need cash so everyone can be paid off. Else the sale won't go through.'

'So what do we do?'

'Easy, really. We just go to the bank, pull some money out and then hand it over to them on the day of the registration.'

'That makes it black money?' It didn't sound too risky so far. Mr M nodded. 'How much money?'

'Thirty-five lakhs.'

'That much! In cash?' I'd never seen more than a lakh in cash and even that was a fat bundle of notes. 'How on earth will we carry that much money around on the day of the sale?'

'Oh, just get a small suitcase from your mother. Any old one we can hand over with the money in it.'

'Ah, and hope no one will realise what's in it when we lurk around outside the land registration office!' I'd seen enough Bollywood movies to know that money was regularly carried around in suitcases in India. I also knew that thieves and muggers had X-ray vision when it came to hard cash stuffed in unusual places. But that was what we did in the end.

The registration office was in the teeming old Fort area of the city and Seller had turned up with his brother as bodyguard, a shifty tobacco-chewing man who I felt sure would try to do a runner with our booty. I was holding so hard onto the suitcase handle, gouges had formed in the palm of my hand. Mr M played the cool customer, a cheque for the 'white' portion sticking casually out of the top of his shirt pocket. The deal had been that the younger couple would get the white money part of our payment (with which they would go off and buy another house) while the old boy would take the cash and use it to build a house on a small plot of land he owned near the railway station.

Son and Daughter-in-Law turned up in the autorickshaw he drove for a living. Our document writer was buzzing around in a state of high excitement, gathering signatures on a plethora of closely typed forms. 'Three-way deal, very difficult,' he said to me as he passed by in a whirl. Everyone else was clearly as nervous as I was. I saw Daughter-in-Law hanging grimly onto the signed document, waiting to ensure it was passed on only when the cheque was handed over. Seller and Brother had also now emerged from their hired car and started circling my precious suitcase.

Son sidled up to me and whispered

something about being given the cash portion as well, which he assured me he would later pass on to his father. I managed to keep my knee from involuntarily kicking outwards and connecting with his shin. Instead I smiled and hissed, 'You hand over the document this minute if you want your cheque. As for the money, it's your father's. Just as the house should have been.'

In a beautifully choreographed move, he grabbed the cheque while his wife gave Mr M the document, their excitement at getting the money making them forget to be shame-faced. The suitcase with the bank notes was handed over to Seller and his brother, who hurriedly took it to the car. I watched them count the bundles while throwing them, one by one, into a hessian rice sack.

The empty suitcase was handed back. Walking back to our car with it rattling beside me, I felt a surge of triumph. I was now the legal owner of my very own hovel.

4

The Architect's office was in posh Kowdiar. An old house with the typical Art Deco flourishes of many houses on Trivandrum's main road. Except here the Art Deco features had been masked by a false wall carrying a clever modernist pattern. I should have taken a cue from it. Some kind of subtle message from a kindly god making frantic gestures in my direction: Beware of Architects Who Build False Walls! But I swanned into the office in similar jolly fashion to Androcles entering the lion's cave.

The room was bare but there were darling little civilising touches: a creeper slung over a bright blue wall (false maybe?) which was visible from the large unbarred window next to me, a rustic earthen urn carrying a collection of colourful and beautifully sharpened pencils, an old stone rice grinder acting as a corner table for a collection of glossy interior design magazines. Everything indicated high taste to me. Architect wore white khadi, had a beard and dreamy eyes and looked like an artist whom we had disturbed in the midst of composing an epic poem. I liked him straightaway.

'Of course one can build next to the sea,' he said, making a dreamy, airy gesture with one hand as he leaned back in his swingy leather chair. 'It will be a beautiful project. We can make you a beautiful seaside home. In fact, we should make your entire garden wall out of toughened glass so that you get the full benefit of the beautiful view.'

Architect had Builder sitting next to him, a large man with a small head supported by a bull neck around which hung a thick gold chain. Correction, a gold *rope*. He had the latest iPhone sticking out of his Ralph Lauren shirt pocket and had placed an iPad Pro on the table before him. So far he had not had much to say but spent the meeting looking at us with a strangely hungry expression on his face. Suddenly, on mention of the glass wall, he spoke up. His voice was surprisingly high-pitched for one who looked like he ate elephant meat.

'We can even build an infinity pool in the back garden so that, when you look out of your patio, you will see nothing but water, water, water.'

He pronounced it 'payshio', which I found unsettling, but I reminded myself sternly that I wasn't in leafy Buckinghamshire. I did not like to diss his idea straightaway. 'Infinity pool? Like those on hotel rooftops? I do rather like those, but we're in the Coastal Regulation Zone,' I reminded the room at large, noticing a querulous little-biddy note creeping into my voice.

The CRZ was a large and complicated piece of legislation drawn up by one of India's more flamboyant environment ministers, which stipulated about ten thousand dos and don'ts for building anything within 500 metres of the high tide line anywhere on India's 7,517 km coastline. I had managed to source a copy of the CRZ which was kept well-hidden on an obscure Ministry of Environment, Forest and Climate Change website and had spent days scouring it to try to make some sense out of what we would legally be allowed. Much to my consternation, I'd discovered that there were not one but *four* Coastal Regulation Zones.

One stretched 4 km out to sea and I ruled this one out with relief as we were certainly building on land, not sea, and had no intention of ejecting 'solid waste' directly out to sea. I tried to ignore the irony that a short kilometre north of our plot lay the government-owned

Travancore Titanium Products Ltd., which pumped an evil yellow frothing liquid directly out into the sea on a daily basis. The acrid stench caused locals to emerge in angry protest every once in a while, but they were easily quietened by offers of jobs in the factory, at which point they swiftly turned from protestors to collaborators.

I also wondered whether to take comfort from the fact that, CRZ or no CRZ, the Kerala government had recently passed a hugely controversial port project led by a Gujarati businessman who was said to be Prime Minister Modi's best friend. So the CRZ was clearly not a document taken very seriously by the people meant to enforce it, hurrah!

To continue the findings of my assiduous research: Zone 1 was ecologically sensitive areas and, yes, I could see the logic in preventing anyone from building plush houses and hotels on top of baby tortoise hatching areas and in the midst of India's last mangrove forests. But that still left Zones 2 and 3, which covered the areas that either had nothing built on them yet or had already been taken over by fishing and other coastal communities. The energetic protests of these communities had caused government lawyers to rewrite parts of the Environment Protection Act which, from what I could see, was a ten-year exercise in muddying the legal waters to an opaque murk. Buildings—even extensions of existing buildings—were allowed in one zone but not the other. However, the occasional use of the word 'authorised' threw in a useful loophole. Useful to those with government connections, I supposed, although if you lacked these connections you would probably be liable for a jail sentence for chancing any transgressions.

(Time for a Reader Challenge. If anyone reading this can manage to work out the difference between Zones 2 and 3 of the CRZ or even track down a definition of the word 'authorised', I guarantee great riches. I spent hours studying the rules, trying to figure out what made one zone different from the other and which one our newly purchased plot sat in, but it was like trying to crack the Enigma code. To this day, 'fuzzy' remains the best word to describe my findings.)

'Ah, rules ... rules,' Architect said in the kind of voice that made me think he was about to recite a sonnet about roses and summer days. 'If we all bothered about rules, we would never achieve anything at all.'

I cast a look at Mr M, who I was sure would get up and flounce out of this elegant office instantly. My British-passport holding Chartered Accountant husband. Upright. Correct. Stuffy even. He was gazing admiringly at Architect as though he had never heard such wisdom in his life.

A week later, we were back in Architect's office to look at the plans he had drawn up. Beautiful sketches of a beautiful house as he had promised (so at least I wasn't wrong in my assessment of his artistic skills). The sketches showed a plush four-bedroom double-storied house with verandas and colonnades and balconies and solar panels. Did I forget to say attached bathrooms? Yes, every bedroom led off into a dressing area and a spacious bathroom. One bathroom showed a dinky little tub, another a shower area open to the skies. It was like something you would expect to see on the Hollywood hills.

'But we're allowed precisely 638 square feet of constructed area,' I reminded the room again. It was odd how my voice had recently adopted a moaning tone. I'd also taken to talking to the walls and furniture because it was clear that, with every utterance, I was attaining less and less eye-contact from the people around me. Nevertheless, I continued undaunted, 'It has to be the same floor area as the house that stood there before, remember? Well, that's according to CRZ rules pertaining to *re*-construction as opposed to *new* construction, which appears in Section xvii of Appendix 72 ...'

Not a soul was listening. Especially not Builder-with-bull-neck who was in fact already headed bullishly out to his Land Rover so we could go to the plot and start measuring. 'Maybe there will even be space for a fifth bedroom,' I thought I heard him say to Mr M over his shoulder, as I trotted in their wake. 'Plus we should see if there's space for that infinity pool ...'

I have to admit it. Something about the can-do-ness of Architect's team was immensely appealing. Especially in a land where heat and humidity conspire to create a kind of ennui that infects everyone from coconut-pickers to CEOs. But I was aware that, once the house was built and the money handed over, this very efficient team would disappear behind innumerable walls (not false but impenetrable definitely) while we faced the wrath of the Corporation bods. And, of course, the only reason the Corporation bods would be interested in us—and be patient enough to wait until we had *completed* building our four-bedroom mansion—would be so that they could extract a vast sum of money from us in order to prevent them from demolishing the entire structure citing non-compliance with the CRZ. *That* was how the system worked. And the government is either naïve or nuts if it thinks it has cut all this out by demonitising old 500- and 1,000-rupee notes. It's the channels of corruption that need blocking off, not filthy lucre, human love for which has been around since Mohenjodaro, most likely.

5

ANYWAY, OFF WE WENT TO TRIVANDRUM Corporation. Mr M and I, that is, not Architect and Builder, who were still retaining their dreamy insouciance towards anything approaching building regulations. Someone had told us (in a comforting tone of voice) that Trivandrum Corporation had smartened up recently, introducing machines and computerised systems designed to keep petty corruption down.

There was a mêlée in the Corporation's minuscule car park where around fifty cars and three hundred two-wheelers were vying for space on an empty plot that last night's rains had turned into a giant bowl of tea. We managed to create a space for our car by half-submerging it behind a floating van and I waded out of the car park, salwar hitched to my knees, to the warm appreciation of the people standing outside the photo-copying shack.

In terms of jam-packedness, the veranda outside the main building was not very much better as everyone who had parked their vehicles in the car park (plus a few others who had wisely chosen to travel by bus instead) were standing around waving papers in the air. It wasn't a riot, merely an Indian queue waiting to be served by somebody whose job description must have stated: 'Unafraid of being stampeded to death'.

After some peering, I spotted three women seated at a desk, barely visible behind mounds of paper. 'What is happening here?' I asked one member of the mêlée.

'Kudumbashree,' he said.

I recognised the name given to a grassroots

scheme that created employment and education opportunities for poor women. Started in 1998 as a community-driven initiative, it grew in pyramid-fashion to become a hugely popular social and entrepreneurial system with over 40 lakh members whose value the government was swift to recognise and embrace. Laudable, of course, except that employment was sometimes ingeniously created simply by inserting a layer of Kudumbashree women into an already overwrought bureaucracy.

'You need to get an application letter from the Kudumbashree desk if it's about house ownership,' my helpful fellow-supplicant said.

'House ownership? Oh, that's a bit of a distant dream right now. I'm here only to get permission to build,' I said.

The man retorted with what sounded like a cross between a snort and a gasp. 'Good luck!' he said, in a heartfelt manner, shaking his head in anticipation of my fate before I found myself sucked, helpless, into the crowd.

Emerging on to the other side of the thicket of arms and bodies, I managed to make eye-contact with one of the women behind the desk. 'I'm not sure I need to be here,' I said. 'Someone told me it's all computerised now.'

She smiled the smile of someone supremely confident in her indispensability. Her voice was firm. 'For *anything* you have to come here first and take a letter from us.'

'And then?'

She sighed. 'Then you have to take a token from the machine inside and go with the token and letter to the desk when the computer calls your number.'

So computers were involved but hadn't taken over the world of Trivandrum Corporation in Orwellian fashion just yet. 'Okay, so may I have a letter please?'

'What is your application for?' In case this sounds like a casual conversation, I should clarify that this woman and I were in fact shouting quite loudly at each other to be heard over the human limb thicket I was now an integral part of. I had to be quick as there was every danger of being sucked right back in.

'House building.'

'Own house?'

I thought it was obvious that one was rather unlikely to queue up on a hot afternoon to get permission to build someone else's house, but I had no desire to fall at the first hurdle by upsetting this helpful woman. 'Own house,' I said obediently.

She was already scribbling in Malayalam on a sheet of dirty white paper. 'Name?'

I gave her my name, spelling out the unfamiliar North Indian surname. 'Mishra,' she said, writing furiously.

'No, no, Misra.'

'That's what I said, 'Mishra.'

'Misra, without an "h".' She sighed again and I thought I detected an eye-roll. I was clearly one of those awkward customers she and her Kudumbashree colleagues moaned about at the water cooler.

She decided it wasn't worth fighting me over something as significant as my name and moved on. 'Address?'

I pulled out a file from the commodious satchel on my shoulder and read out the address from the registration document. I had taken to carrying every single scrap of paper generated by the house purchase so far; it was an impressive pile that I heaved around, camel-like, just in case anyone needed this document or that. I was not going to be caught out document-less in a crisis.

The woman clicked her tongue in irritation at my accent and stretched out her hand to read it for herself. Painstakingly, she copied the address on to her letter. The letter was in Malayalam anyway so she could have been spelling everything with a few extra 'h's' thrown in for all I knew.

'Revenue stamp,' she said, clicking her fingers at me.

'Was I supposed to have brought a revenue

stamp?' I enquired in dismay. We had come so far, it would be a crying shame to turn away for want of something that was no more than 2 sq. cm in size. 'I haven't got a revenue stamp,' I said, trying not to hang my head in shame. What was the point of carrying all those documents around if I hadn't had the sense to slip a sheaf of revenue stamps in with them? Every Indian carries a pack of revenue stamps around in their back pockets on a just-in-case basis.

The nice young woman in a headscarf, clearly trying to help, gave me a withering look which made it clear that I had already, at 10 a.m., taken the prize for Most Difficult Customer of the Day. Then, shaking her head in amazement at her own patience with my audacity, she opened her drawer and rummaged around a bit before emerging with a tiny scrap of red stamp clutched between thumb and forefinger. She licked the back of the stamp, stuck it down at the bottom of the letter and then, tapping it, said, 'Sign.'

'On top of the stamp?'

'Yesss,' she sighed in an I-really-need-that-coffee-now manner.

And so I did, feeling the warmth of her spittle under my right hand but utterly grateful for this life-saving act. 'Now?'

'*Now* computer,' she said, waggling her head in the direction of the door. If I had ever feared that computers would take over the world, this young woman was proof that it hadn't happened yet and probably never would. Oddly, I felt reassured at the thought that she would lay down her life if the battle between Man and Computer ever came to the doors of Trivandrum Corporation.

Inside, there was bedlam of another sort. 'Token, token,' the guard at the door said, waving at me frantically as I made for the nearest desk. I looked at where he pointed and saw three colour-coded machines lined up. One said, 'Tax', the other, 'Birth & Death', the third 'Electricity/Water Bill'. None mentioned House

Building Permissions. Maybe Architect had been right after all. One didn't need permission to build houses in Kerala, they just emerged from the earth like lots of happy mushrooms.

I went back to the guard. 'Where do I go for a token for permission to build a house?'

'Where is the plot?' he asked.

'Veli.'

'Your own purchased plot or family plot?'

I was pretty sure none of this was information the guard needed to guide me to the right counter. But if there's one characteristic that marks out the Malayali, it is curiosity. If you stop to ask for directions to a street, the Malayali will inevitably ask you who you're going to meet there. Or, if you ask for someone by name, they will enquire the nature of your business with them. I had tried to explain this to Mr M once. It was something to do with Kerala's general prosperity and its people not having anything really grave (like famine or starvation) to worry about. He had not been convinced but that was only because he came from the famine-struck, starving north.

Once Security Guard and I had exchanged the names of our maternal grandmothers and full postal details, he informed me in a conspiratorial manner that I was to go to Counter 24. This, I felt sure, was not information he freely dished out to anyone but his best friends. I gave him the kind of subtle nod collaborators use and scuttled off.

Counter 24 was a small desk manned by a fierce-looking woman (it was the moustache on her upper lip that leads me, in fact, to use the verb 'manned'). When I told her what I wanted, she gave me a derisive look, so I gathered that punters seeking permission to build houses were scum of the earth in her opinion.

'*Why* do you want to build?' she asked me.

We were straying into a rather existentialist area and I wasn't sure she wanted to hear the whole saga about economic recessions and the consequent migratory patterns of humans. 'Er ... we want a house here in Kerala?' I ventured, unsure of why I should sound so apologetic.

'To live permanently?' She gave me a piercing stare as though warning me of the consequences of such a rash act.

'Not permanently. We usually live in London ... so we may come when it gets cold there ... etc.' I trailed off, unsure of whether I was digging myself into a hole that would soon become my (and my house plan's) grave.

So far no mention had been made of the dreaded CRZ even though she could see the name 'Veli' on the top of the file. Everyone knew Veli was a coastal area but there was a slim possibility that this would escape Trivandrum Corporation's notice.

'You fill in these forms,' she said, pulling out half a dozen sheets of paper from a series of pigeon-holes next to her desk.

'Now?'

'Of course now. But if you want to come again tomorrow, you can come again tomorrow. What should it matter to me?'

Seeing that this was a rhetorical (if stinging) question, I did not answer it but scurried off, chastened, to find a quiet corner to fill my forms. A plastic chair was lying around, miraculously empty. I looked at the forms. Everything was in Malayalam, so I got up and slunk my way back to Moustache Woman's desk. 'So sorry, but do you have English versions of these forms?'

'English forms?'

I nodded nervously.

'Forms in *English*?'

I nodded again, remembering too late how chauvinistic most Malayalis are about their language. She picked up a file from the file-tower on her desk and started leafing through it. I tried to work out if I'd been dismissed. But she hadn't finished with me just yet. 'This is Kerala. People who can't write Malayalam should not be living here.' She was looking into her file as she muttered this and it was perfectly possible she was not addressing me at all. A bit like that time my friend's mother—a dignified black woman of Afro-Caribbean descent—heard a white woman in a shop say, 'I wonder when they will all go back to their own countries.' No eye-contact, no direct insult. Just a few words strung politely together to make you feel unwanted.

It isn't as if home-grown Malayalis do not like anyone from their far-flung diaspora returning to the homeland. Returnees, particularly those from the Gulf countries, are welcomed and admired even, for the wealth they bring back and invest in businesses and religious establishments and the madly colourful houses that punctuate every highway. But these returnees are people who took Kerala with them when they left its shores, zealously retaining the language and culture until they got back home. They were nothing like me: second-generation 'foreigners' from whom the Malayaliness had gradually leached out and nearly disappeared. We spoke funny, wore the wrong clothes, had weird attitudes, were suspected of looking down our noses at everything to do with Kerala ...

I slunk back to my corner, feeling about two-foot high, and squinted again at the forms. Luckily, one of my grandmothers had suffered from that same brand of Malayali chauvinism and had attempted to hammer into her three foreign grandchildren a few elements of their heritage. I had spent one entire summer holiday at Ammumma's house keeping a Malayalam tutor (and all the neighbourhood kids) in a state of high amusement at my learning efforts. I am proud to say that, by the end of that four-week holiday, I had picked up enough Malayalam to read cinema posters and bus boards, only so slowly that the bus was usually disappearing down the bottom of the road by the time I'd worked out its destination.

'Letter by letter,' I told my panicking heart, starting a word only to forget the first few letters by the time I'd figured out the last. Malayalam loves long words. And silly palindromes.

Mr M, leaning over, bumped me with his shoulder in an affectionate gesture and said sympathetically, 'It isn't in the least bit like Hindi, is it?'

'D-r-a-v-i-d-i-a-n. Remember?' I snapped. 'Different family of languages entirely. Different people, different ethnicity, different customs. Which is why you Aryans drove us down the Indian peninsula in the first place. Remember? And now *you* want to come and live *here*. It might be an idea to ask the locals first if they want you here. Polite even.'

It was not sensible to vent my annoyance on him, or even on his bloodthirsty ancestors from a few millennia ago, but I was feeling very peeved. In fact, I had been feeling peeved for a few weeks now and, finally, he and Moustache Woman had given me a chance to unload.

6

We drove past Veli Tourist Village on our way to the plot, the main gate fringed cheerily with plastic-toy and tender-coconut sellers. Already a few tourist buses had pulled up and people were queuing to buy entrance tickets. I wanted to lean my head out of the car window to tell them they could take the lane past our plot to the beach and make their way into the tourist village from there without paying a rupee. But that would have robbed the government of the income they so desperately needed to maintain the place. Not that maintenance seemed very high priority, given that the beach stayed pitch dark (due to a tussle between the Electricity and Tourism Boards about who would pay for the lights) and the dangerously cracked walkway, which had taken a terrible battering in the last monsoon. Its railings had rusted and turned to delicate brown filigree and some bits had fallen away completely. But the domestic tourists whom Kerala Tourism was wooing so energetically still came, posing against mossy statues and rusty railings to photograph each other in God's Own Country. Never mind that Kerala Tourism's catchphrase had recently been hijacked by a group campaigning against the stray dog menace to become Dog's Own Country. What the tourists from distant states were guaranteed was our sea and this—vast and blue and seemingly endless—unerringly cast its spell to ensure that they came again and again, if for nothing else than to gaze rapt at its ever-changing beauty.

That morning, it lay calm as though breathing lightly in sleep while fishermen squatted on the beach, mending their nets.

Our plot too was humming pleasurably with activity. Three workers were putting up the wall I had designed, stacking breeze blocks one on top of the other and pasting them into small pillars with cement mix. Four other workers were noisily engaged in making a giant brick structure right next to the gate. Builder was stomping around, doing his bull-in-a-pen thing and shouting at everyone in sight. He stopped on seeing us and gave us a rare and rather beautiful smile. We had, after all, just paid a vast sum of money into his bank in order to get the construction started.

'What's that?' I asked him, pointing to the large brick structure.

'That will be the store for construction materials, cement bags, etc.,' he replied.

'Gosh, it looks more like a house than a store. Does it have to be so big?' My mother's guest room, in which we had been living for a few months now, wasn't half as capacious as this house we were making for a bunch of cement bags.

'When it is being made, we should make it big enough to fit everything. Don't worry, it will be demolished at the end of the project.'

That sounded wasteful to me, but I could see that Builder did nothing by halves. I had to be grateful he wasn't building an aircraft hangar.

'Tomorrow we will start demolishing the old house so that, by next week, we can prepare the land and make the foundation for the new construction,' he said.

I felt a frisson of excitement. We had finally managed to get permission from Trivandrum Corporation to build a house on our plot. It wasn't going to be anything like the mansion that Architect had drawn on our earlier visits, but a modest one-bedroom house whose footprint matched that of the old house. I was satisfied with this and tried to ignore Architect's reassuring words to Mr M. 'One can always expand later,' he had said, dropping his voice to keep me out of it as I had by now clearly established myself in his mind as The Enemy, mean and parsimonious and always carping on about Rules. I ignored him as I wasn't going to worry about 'later' when I had a fair bit on my plate in the here and now.

As a matter of fact, demolishing the old house to build afresh had not expressly been allowed, but Architect had explained a cunning plan to demolish all but one wall of the old house so that, when Corporation bods swung by, there was still enough of the old house left to convince them that this was a rebuild rather than a fresh build. This entire supposition felt a little flawed to me as it was based on the assumption that everyone in the Planning Department of Trivandrum Council was a little weak in the head. But when I expressed this fear to Mr M, he reminded me of how a little palm-greasing was all it would take if we were ever faced with the unlikely problem of Trivandrum Corporation's Planning Department supervisors possessing a few brain cells between them. I found it worrying how a few weeks in Kerala had Mr M using terms like 'palm grease' so nonchalantly.

Two days later, when a rather enthusiastic bulldozer was brought into the plot, I could see that not one inch of the old house was likely to be conserved, leave alone a whole wall. It was a demolition in every sense of the word and, when the deed was done and the dust settled, the plot looked like a war zone minus the bodies. Not even a brick of the old house had been left standing. Everything had been smashed to smithereens.

There was little one could do and, by this stage, I too had started to feel a little gung-ho. As far as feelings go, it was a bloody infectious one.

One small problem remained. After demolishing an old house where did one get rid of the debris? In fact, where did one get rid of even the tiniest bag of household garbage these days in Trivandrum? There was no waste disposal system at all in the city. A process that the world's biggest and most populous cities manage in numerous cunning ways had, here in sleepy little Trivandrum, become a colossal and seemingly intractable problem leading to what I saw as a near breakdown of civilised society.

The story goes thus: a few years ago, Trivandrum Corporation had built a garbage disposal plant in a village called Velapilsaala on the outskirts of the city. Within a few months, however, the locals had started protesting about the stench and the cockroaches, even claiming that nobody would marry their girls when they heard they were from the filthy dump-town of Velapilsaala. When the villagers found their protests being ignored, they took matters into their own hands and barricaded the town, lying across the roads, Tiananmen Square style, in order to block the path of Trivandrum Corporation's garbage trucks. These truck drivers instantly downed tools, probably seized by a fit of socialist solidarity but claiming that they feared for their lives, and there seemed to be little the authorities could do by way of a solution after this. They had therefore, in good-governance fashion, thrown up their hands and more or less told the hapless citizens of Trivandrum to manage their garbage disposal themselves.

Some Resident Welfare Associations had hired people to do a door-to-door collection of household waste but, from what I had observed in my mother's locality, these people merely gathered all the rubbish on the quietest street in the area and proceeded to burn it there. Many people, refusing to pay for this, took to burning garbage in their own backyards and the air was always hung with thin curtains of acrid smoke. Gradually, every street in this once pretty town had grown its own personal garbage mountain: stinking stacks of plastic bottles and polystyrene cartons and food waste that, of course, then attracted rats and stray dogs.

To the latter—emaciated creatures forced to live by their wits—these garbage heaps had come as manna from heaven and, as a consequence, most streets now had a resident squad of strays that were apparently known to attack early-morning walkers who they assumed, quite naturally, were slinking along in the furtive dawn-light in order to recover lost garbage. No one was allowed to harm these dogs or even cart them away as they were protected by animal rights warrior and Union Minister Maneka Gandhi, who was way more terrifying than the fiercest of them. When protests in Kerala grew, Maneka Gandhi claimed that vast sums of money had been paid to the Animal Welfare Board in Kerala in order to sterilise the stray dogs, hinting at the misappropriation of funds by the Communists. But, after a sixty-five-year-old woman was killed by a pack of dogs in Pullivilla near Trivandrum, the Kerala government proposed to cull these creatures. While Maneka Gandhi's new-found power at the Centre would normally have put an immediate end to any such plans, this was (and still is) complicated somewhat by the BJP continuing to eye in some puzzlement its dismal election prospects in Kerala. What was the killing of a few dogs when compared to this grand project?

Caught in this Mad Max world of feral dogs and piles of garbage taller than houses, I was filled with sudden nostalgia for the brown (biodegradable), green (paper) and blue (bottles and cans) bins that Southwark Council had assigned to me in what now seemed like a distant heaven. Those beautiful containers would be sitting there neatly on my driveway back in London while I skulked around the streets of Trivandrum trying to find a quiet spot to hurl a bag of eggshells and vegetable peelings unseen.

As for the good folk of Trivandrum ... I was fast coming to the conclusion that the dwellers of this town were saintly beings who simply put on their blinkers and halos every morning before arming themselves with a stout stick and stepping out of their houses to sail through life, picking their way through heaps of garbage and dodging murderous canines along the way.

7

If there's one thing Mr M excels at, it is keeping accounts and calculating awkward numbers and generally tabulating stuff. He is an accountant after all and, according to his mother, was born clutching a spreadsheet in one chubby fist.

He was now gazing with satisfaction at his laptop, jabbing at the calculator every now and then as though poking someone in the eye. Rubbing his hands, he got up and announced with an air of evil satisfaction, 'I'm going to get the bastard.'

'Pardon?'

'Bloody Builder's been ripping us off.

There's a great big gaping hole of 1.5 lakh rupees in this budget. I did think the figure he'd quoted in his estimate was way off the mark. But I've got him now. By the goolies.'

I'm a peaceable soul and the language of conflict never fails to make me uneasy. What I didn't know, however, was that I should have been hearing the great big clangs of warning bells going off in my head at that point. Instead, I dismissed the little chill that had stepped onto my spine with plans to descend it and returned to my book.

It started with a detailed but polite email. And a similar sort of reply. Hubby to Builder and then Builder to Hubby. At first the emails were a daily affair and then they became twice daily. They got less and less polite. Then came the phone calls. If you could still describe them as 'calls' once the volume had escalated to levels beyond those normally employed in conversation.

Alongside all that, work on-site came to a

swift halt. When we visited, what we found was a plot that now had an unpainted compound wall and gate but what it protected was a half-built security cabin (the name that had been affectionately conferred on the giant shed for cement bags that had been made by Builder before he had stopped feeling that affectionate). This cabin stood on a mammoth foundation, had head-height walls but only holes for windows and the great open skies of Kerala where there should have been a roof. There was that and, of course, a heap of rubble where there once had stood a house. Had anyone told me then that I would one day mourn the passing of the fisherman's old yellow hovel with its mouldy sagging walls and cracked floor weeping sand, I would have been incredulous. But I did. Simply because its existence had allowed me to think of my 'house by the sea' which was, all said and done, marginally better than my pile of rubble by the sea.

Builder was intractable. Unless we paid him a vast sum of money, he would keep his workers away. Mr M was intractable as well, saying that more money would be paid only when the accrued shortfall was made up or at least acknowledged so that it could be made up later.

So off we went to Architect, who said some dreamy things about non-paying customers that merely enraged Mr M further.

'He's protecting that bloody builder!' he said, storming out of the elegant office and jumping into the car.

'Well, what do you expect? He's known Builder a lot longer than he's known us.' I grabbed at the armrest as we screeched out of the car park.

'But that isn't how it works! As an architect, he's supposed to be an honest broker between builder and client. Not operating hand in glove with an unscrupulous builder!'

'So what do we do?' My question was

drowned in the blare of the car horn. Mr M's thumb was now glued to the horn and he was yelling a Hindi obscenity at a motorcyclist, who promptly mouthed a Malayalam obscenity back. I was the only person who understood both.

'No question in my mind,' Mr M replied, finally ungluing his finger. 'Tomorrow we find another architect and builder.'

I didn't think I ought to ask any more questions until we had stopped weaving crazily through the evening traffic to reach the safety of my mother's home.

8

BUILDER HAD ANOTHER PLAN FOR US, HOWEVER. It started with the heavies. They came to the plot, a gang of men clad in vests and lungis, moustachioed in a way only Malayalis can be.

For anyone who has not seen Malayalam movies, I should explain that a ferocious tash and lungi-vest is stock uniform for a baddie, just in case the viewers failed to pick up on all the other cues contained in the script. In Kerala's complex social system, the lungi stands (or, more correctly, falls) at the wrong end of the scale from the starched white dhoti of aristocrats, while the double-stitched, equally colourful kaili occupies a strange middle-ground, worn by upper-class men in the privacy of their homes on steamy afternoons, presumably because of its swift disrobability (precisely one second, I was once informed by an older female cousin who, during my teenage years, played the role of mentor and guide in all matters relating to my sexual development).

Lungis/kailis are nothing more than two metres of madly printed cloth, worn wrapped around the waist and folded up and over. How this ensemble ever survives a film fight sequence without falling right off is one of gravity's biggest unsolved mysteries and one that Malayali men the world over guard fiercely.

For a brief time in the '70s, women appropriated the lungi as a fashion item but that quickly gave way to the delights of the daytime nightie, which deserves a whole chapter of its own. For now I shall only say in its defence that in Kerala the day-nightie forms part of a long feminist journey from those best-forgotten days when women were expected to show their respect for older and/or higher caste men by dropping their loosely worn top cloths in order to bare their breasts (I promise I'm not lying).

Anyway, cutting back to the present, the lungi-clad heavies stood at our gate and shouted a lot about not having been paid by us for their hard labour. Never mind that we had never once seen any one of these men actually working on our plot. We tried to tell them that we had already paid Builder and that it was his responsibility to pay his workers since they had been hired by him. I recognised the man who had supervised work on our plot. Most of the people with him, however, were merely rabble-rousers. And rouse the rabble they did.

In Kerala, the socialist identity is a powerful force and it never takes long for a crowd to gather and speak with one loud voice. Reminiscent of the good vs evil narratives of

Kathakali performances that people stayed up till midnight to watch in temple compounds, these rich vs poor spectacles have become the stuff of street entertainment and, often, financial reward. The big, wealthy expat refusing to pay the poor labourer's hard-earned wages—I girded my loins, readying myself for the role of Putana or some other Chief Baddie.

Curiously, however, it soon became apparent that a large number of our neighbours were taking our side. Either we'd already grown more popular than we were aware of, or we were the neighbourhood's future bankers/ moneylenders/do-gooders who mustn't, at any cost, be chased away. Whatever the reason, I could not help a small swell of pride at having been pulled thus to the community's collective bosom. It made me feel almost tearful, in fact.

Even more surprised than I, however, were the visiting rabble-rousers and it wasn't long before they were shouting at our neighbours too. Two unlikely factions were forming and, hallelujah, we were on the more populous, winning side. Just as suddenly as they had come, the visiting team decided there was more dignity in retreat and so they left on their motorcycles, trailing clouds of diesel in their wake.

We may have won a minor victory, but clearly things weren't going to stay quiet for very long. Our house construction had hit the buffers and screeched to a halt, but the pace of our lives had conversely and quite suddenly been upped to a near-manic level.

9

SURE ENOUGH, THE NEXT DAY WE RECEIVED A PHONE call from the ASI of Valiathura Police Station. He said a complaint had been filed against us and we would therefore have to attend the police station at 10 o'clock the following morning.

As another Kerala day dawned, we left for the police station, armed with my satchel of papers and a file full of Mr M's spreadsheets. Neither of us had ever received a summons from the constabulary before so my feelings as we stepped into the cop-shop were an odd mix of righteousness and plain old fear. It was larger than most police stations I'd seen from the outside, on two floors and with a number of 'hearing' rooms on the ground floor.

The ASI who was due to hear our case looked about twenty years old but, almost as though needing to make up for such an unfortunate shortfall in age, he sported the meanest, toughest expression I have seen any cop wear (and that includes cops on the many American TV serials I have watched). I received not even the glimmer of a smile in response to my greeting and sunk back in my plastic seat, chastened. Outside, in the sunlit car park, I saw Builder's SUV pull up. He had three or four people with him, and I recognised a couple of the hoods who had recently visited us. They pretended as though they had not seen us, which was a charade that rather suited me. Their forced camaraderie and joshing did not convince me either.

I watched while the ASI and another young policeman in the next cubicle went through case after case, mostly related to petty crime and domestic violence. And then it was our turn.

Builder was summoned from the car park as he was the chief complainant. In a long, rambling monologue, he stated in essence that we had not paid him for the diligent high-class services he had scrupulously rendered. He looked nervous now, licking his lips and attempting unsuccessfully to steady his voice. His unease was strange, given that all this was his idea in the first place, but I don't suppose he had benefitted from elocution lessons in whatever borstal he had attended as a schoolboy. I wondered if I ought to feel sorry for him before sternly instructing my heart to desist from bleeding unnecessarily. At one point, the ASI asked him to hurry up. This distraction seemed to make Builder dry up completely and so his narrative came to an abrupt halt. It was our turn now. As Mr M was the main accused, the ASI wanted to interview him, but I was asked to sit alongside to play interpreter.

The ASI gestured towards Builder, seated next to me. 'Is what this man says true?' he enquired.

'It is true that we had appointed him as our builder. Or rather, the architect we had appointed recommended him,' I replied.

'And has he done all the work he claims to have done?'

'Yes, that he has.'

'And has he been paid anything by you?'

At this point, Mr M swung into Chartered Accountant mode, pulling out carefully numbered and serialised spreadsheets, all of them dated and with counterfoils of cheque leaves attached.

I saw the ASI's eyes glaze over. Clearly, it was an inability with maths that had sent him in the direction of the police services rather than an office job. But he politely picked up paper after paper and scanned them with glassy eyes. Then, looking slightly queasy, he barked at Builder.

'Then why did you say they have not paid you anything? What are all these cheques, einh?'

Builder seemed terribly in need of a chapstick. Licking his lips, he croaked, 'I did not say they did not pay *anything* ...'

'That was exactly what you said,' the ASI snapped.

'No sir,' Builder wheedled, 'I said they did not *complete* the payment ...'

'Yes, but you have not completed their job, have you? How much are you saying they owe you for the work that has been done so far?'

'Sir, maybe it is fifty-sixty thousand rupees ...'

'What do you mean "maybe"? Is it fifty or is it sixty?'

'Sir ...'

'You don't know, do you? You haven't done any calculations or kept any records or receipts like this, have you?' He shook Mr M's file under Builder's nose while I hastily translated for Mr M's benefit.

'Sir, all I know is that they owe me money and ...'

'What do you mean "owe money"? Is this not money they have already paid you? And, if they owe you more money, then you have to have some way of proving that.' He tapped on a cheque counterfoil before delivering his Parthian shot. 'What you are really saying is, why is all their money not sitting in my pocket, aren't you?'

I wanted to stand up and cheer this marvellous policeman. Maths may not have been his strong point, but he sure had an excellent instinct for human behaviour, figuring out in a matter of seconds which side to vent his wrath on. Plus he did brilliant speeches.

Builder looked sulky and scuffed at the wooden desk with one giant sandal. But the ASI was only just warming to his task. Terrier-like, he carried on wiggling the topic he had caught in his mouth as though it were an annoying rat. He raised his voice a notch. 'And what do you think we, the police, are here for? To have our time wasted by people like you? Can you not see how busy we are here? With all these people who are in genuine trouble. Not opportunists using the name of the police to frighten law-abiding people like these. Filing useless cases.'

I wasn't sure I would have awarded us with such a sweeping appellation as 'law-abiding people'. There had, after all, been that suitcase full of notes and the odd speeding offence and maybe a couple of jumped lights on deserted roads at midnight but it was rather lovely to hear us described thus by the local fuzz and I duly fluffed up my feathers. I couldn't help throwing Builder a sideways triumphant look, but he had gone red in the face and got up with a screech of his chair.

Both sides had to sign a giant register stating that the case had been heard and concluded and then were thrown out of the

ASI's office without further ado. Outside, in the dusty compound, Builder rounded up his now not-so-merry band and they drove off speedily in the SUV but not without throwing us a filthy look first. Despite the triumph, I felt a shiver of apprehension shimmy down my spine.

10

OUR SEARCH FOR ANOTHER CONSTRUCTION TEAM LED us to an old friend of my uncle's. This architect had designed a small block of flats developed on Uncle's ancestral property but his area of specialisation was high-rise construction rather than small homes. Nevertheless, we were assured we would get a straight-talking man, which seemed like the most important quality at the moment.

Architect 2 was small and energetic, dashing about his office like a flibbertigibbet. I have in more languid moments wondered exactly what a flibbertigibbet is, but that was the first word that sprang to mind on meeting this busy, cheerful man. He could, it appeared, take in three or four bits of information delivered by three or four different people (some in his office and others on his constantly ringing pair of mobile phones), in the midst of which he shot instructions at various harried-looking colleagues. He was definitely not composing poetry in his head (à la Architect 1) but using it to store endless amounts of technical and architectural information. Despite being a bit exhausting to watch, he looked likely to be a vast improvement on our last experience.

The office too was not a patch on Architect 1's in design stakes, but there was an inherent honesty in the chaos of skewed furniture and desks piled high with papers. Nothing had been artfully arranged in advance of our visit and there wasn't a false wall in sight. Architect 2 was clearly too busy for stylistic flummery and, from what I could see, had a long client list, many of whom were now crowding the waiting area.

Most reassuring was that Architect 2 was not only familiar with Trivandrum Corporation's Planning Department, he cared enough about rules to have a dedicated member of staff to be his liaison person with said Department. His back-of-an-envelope budget too came in way below the one presented by Architect 1. And he only talked about a plain and sustainable beach house, without mentioning infinity pools once. I was starting to like him more and more.

True, he frowned deeply at us over his round glasses when we told him that we had demolished the old house when all we had permission for was renovation rather than a new build, but I accepted the scolding as though the demolition had been my nefarious plan all along. He also shared my abiding respect for CRZ and all such legislation. Here, finally, was the trusty, upstanding project-partner I had been looking for.

After we put him in the picture about

our stalled construction, he agreed to have a chat with Architect 1 to ensure there was no professional toe-treading. Then he would redesign the building in keeping with the plan sanctioned by Trivandrum Corporation and also find us a new builder. There should be no further delays if we were to beat the monsoons. After that meeting, I went home and had the deepest afternoon nap I had enjoyed in a long time.

11

THE PROJECT RESTARTED AS SOON AS A NEW BUILDER was found. The monsoons were anticipated in two months' time and, ideally, the roof needed to be cast before the deluge swept across the Indian Ocean to crash-land onto Kerala's southern shores. Besides, Architect 2 was anxious about Corporation officials visiting the site and finding out that the old house had been demolished. 'We must act fast,' he said. Plain words but they had the ring of Beethoven's fifth symphony in my ears.

The days were hot and muggy, but a team was found who were willing to start work early and, once again, we started making twice daily trips to supervise.

A small diversion might be necessary at this point to explain to the uninitiated a uniquely Kerala concept called *nokku kooli*, conferred on the hapless citizens of the state by past Communist governments, this being one of the few states in the world that regularly and democratically elects Communists to power. Directly translated, the term 'nokku kooli' means 'looking wage' but, in practice, this is the right that is claimed by all local head-load workers' unions to unload any materials being delivered on their patch. Even if the purchaser/contractor should wish to decline this service, or use their own labour, the union retains the right to claim the money for ... you got it ... merely looking on. And thus, thanks to election sops offered by Communist parties, anyone living in the state is bound to pay a 'looking wage' or nokku kooli for all variety of materials that need to be unloaded at construction or business premises.

Now, Malayalis being generally a peaceable

kind of people (Mr M prefers my quivering amygdala theory) have for long accepted this practice as a necessary evil. But Mr M—whose antecedents lie in the feudal North and whose paternal uncles were all Army Generals and Colonels—could not believe he needed to fall in line with this decades-old practice put in place by 'Bleeding Commies'. My own father and uncles had, in fact, been Communist hotheads in their youth and this was at least part of the reason why Mr M spat the word out with such scorn.

On the day that the roof tiles for the security cabin arrived, the ragtag 'union' who were mostly just the local layabouts, collected silently at our gate, a bit like vultures gathering when an animal has died.

'Six rupees per tile,' the leader said, chewing on his tobacco in suitably surly fashion.

'Tell him to fuck off,' Mr M said.

Translating rapid-fire into Malayalam was tricky at the best of times and my vocabulary did not stretch to cussing. Besides, this was one of those dreaded head-load workers' unions and there was my amygdala to take into consideration.

'He says six rupees is too high,' I said to the man in a weak voice.

'That's the standard rate. Pay it or we will block the unloading.'

'What do you mean "block the unloading"?' I queried, still ever so polite.

'You cannot get anyone else to unload,' the man warned, glaring daggers at the tempo driver, who instantly put his hands into the air with a 'Not me guv' gesture. We were on our own.

That was when I remembered. 'But you cannot prevent the owners from doing their own unloading, can you?'

'*He* will unload?' the union leader asked. Had he been British, the word 'wuss' would no doubt have been employed as a disparaging suffix to that sentence, but the man merely cast a contemptuous look in Mr M's direction.

'Yes, he will,' I replied. In a rush of uncharacteristic courage, I added, 'And so will I.'

A ripple of amusement passed through the crowd. Translating this exchange to Mr M, I proceeded to close the gate and very deliberately lock it. I'd heard rumours of ugly fights and knifings when headload workers' unions were thwarted, but something about the man's arrogance had temporarily switched the fear centre in my amygdala off. In full view of the crowd, Mr M and I proceeded to unload the contents of the tempo into our compound. 1200 tiles, 30 seconds per tile (because they were made of fragile terracotta and had to be carried one by one to the far side of the gate), it took all of 5 hours.

As people on the fringes of the crowd started to mutter and drift away after an hour of this display of Misra Power, the union leader seemed to lose his bluster as well, dropping his lungi and looking foolish and snapping at some of the complainers who were clearly dissatisfied with his atrocious bargaining skills.

Mr M and I carried on into the evening, unloading tile after tile until my fingers were sore and my back aching. But the pile of tiles in the compound was growing reassuringly and the steel bottom of the back of the tempo was gradually becoming visible. At 6 p.m., we were done. Then we opened the gate, ushered the pusillanimous driver into his seat and waved the tempo off.

Only two men were left by this stage, sitting on their haunches and shooting the breeze and one of them nodded almost indiscernibly in my direction. There may have been a glint of something resembling respect in his eyes.

12

ONE BLAZING BLUE AFTERNOON NOT LONG AFTER, I got a phone call.

'Jaishree Misra?'

'Yes, speaking.'

'My name is Sabu Thomas. I am a journalist and environmentalist.'

I was accustomed to getting calls from journalists and was usually delighted to give them my attention. 'How can I help?' I asked.

'You are building a house at Veli, Trivandrum?'

'Yes.'

'There is a problem with that.' His tone shifted up a gear and took on a sinister edge at this point, even though the overall tone was carefully cheesy. 'I believe you have *demolished* the house that stood there before. And are building a *new* construction. That is not allowed as per CRZ rules. Do you know that?'

My old friend CRZ. I knew it was only a matter of time before the old boy resurfaced.

'Okay, but what is it to you, may I ask, Mr Thomas?'

'I told you, I am an environmentalist. I cannot abide people like you destroying our environment like this. I am going to put in a complaint to Trivandrum Corporation.'

Today was clearly a day for old friends. First CRZ and now Trivandrum Corporation.

'Well, if that's the case, Mr Thomas, why are you calling me?'

'I wanted to give you warning.'

'Warning? Well, I appreciate that but if you wish to complain, then complain you must.'

'You have nothing more to say?'

'No. Goodbye.'

I hung up wondering if I should have taken (in fact, grabbed with both hands) the opening that had clearly been given of offering to meet the man with a few fat brown paper envelopes stuffed in my back pocket. But I congratulated myself on my sharp and decisive action.

The next day, he was back. This time calling on Mr M's phone, the conversation taking an eerily similar path. Maybe he thought Mr M and I didn't talk to each other anymore—a sensible enough assumption to make given we'd been building a house together for some months now; the sort of project that often cuts a straight path to the divorce courts. Or maybe he merely wanted to see if Mr M was made of weaker stuff than me. To which I would have said 'Fat chance' had I been in the vicinity. Anyway, he soon found that out for himself as the call was shorter, terser and, if I'm not mistaken, ended with the words, 'So you can fuck off.'

Over the next few days, we tried to dismiss

the calls as being, if not prank-ish, then merely opportunistic. We were fairly certain Builder 1 had something to do with the matter. After all, I'd painstakingly taught him everything there was to know about the CRZ. But I'd be lying if I said that the next call we received was totally unexpected.

It was mid-morning when the site supervisor called. He was so overwrought that he made no sense at first. Gradually, a couple of words started to emerge from the torrent and these were: 'stay order'. These two little words would come to be engraved on my heart in letters of blood in the weeks to come, but I didn't know that then.

Apparently, a man from Trivandrum Corporation had driven up on a motorcycle and—when the supervisor had shown him a photocopy of the plans and permissions—had proceeded to measure the foundation of the half-built house before scribbling on a generic form words to the effect that we had exceeded the permission granted by four feet. Four feet. In terms of a transgression, it was laughable. But, since bribery and corruption had not been involved, four feet might as well have been four miles. We had managed so far to not grease a single outstretched palm and so a stay order was what we deserved.

Now, if a stay order was that easy to impose, it ought (by all the rules of rationality) to be just as easy to waive. But everyone to whom we narrated our sorry saga said roughly this: 'Stay order? *Stay order*!? From the *Corporation*? Very bad, very bad, very, *very* difficult to remove. You're sure? *Stay order!?*' This statement was always accompanied by shakes of the head and death-face grimaces.

Since greasing palms was out of the question, we decided to resort to the lesser evils of nepotism.

An old friend happened to be the most senior bureaucrat in the Kerala government. He was our best bet—approachable and honest—and so we went to his house one evening. His wife brought out glasses of chilled lime juice and a bowl filled with delicate curls of salted banana chips. We told them our tale of woe. He took a deep breath and grimaced in death-face fashion. Then he shook his head slowly. 'Stay order from Trivandrum Corporation. This is going to be very, *very* difficult.'

I could feel a deep gloom envelop me. If the Chief Secretary of Kerala could not save us, then no one could. But I knew CS to be a confident, fearless sort, with a reputation for possessing a very short fuse for incompetence and corruption. And so, unsurprisingly really, his next words were, 'But we shall find a way. People shouldn't be allowed to get away with such low cunning. A quality Kerala specialises in, by the way. Let me talk to the Secretary of the Corporation first. New chap. Tamilian. Honest to a fault.'

After a short conversation on his phone,

CS turned to us, sounding rueful. 'Well, the Secretary's offered to meet you. But he didn't sound too full of hope. Apparently there's a very long process involved in clearing a stay order, including a public hearing in which both sides are required to present statements and make depositions. In Malayalam,' he added, looking significantly in my direction. 'Doesn't help that the Secretary is so young and so new to everything that he's a stickler for procedures. Won't budge an inch this way or that.'

13

AND THUS WE WERE BACK AT TRIVANDRUM Corporation. Only this time, it wasn't to the friendly, enveloping Kudumbashree scrum on the veranda, nor to my old mate the security guard, but straight up to the first floor where the grandees of the Corporation occupy their high pedestals.

The Secretary's office was capacious and looked a bit like a miniature court room with rows and rows of chairs all facing an enormous desk. Dwarfed behind this desk sat the Secretary, a small man who looked about twenty years old. It was scary how all the officials I had recently come up against, and who seemingly held my fate in the palms of their hands, looked like they were barely out of school. The Secretary spoke quickly and confidently.

'I have looked up your case,' he said, 'and I should tell you that your complainant is politically very well connected. Connected to the Corporation Councillors in fact. So your chances of getting the stay order waived are not good. Not good at all.'

'May I ask who he is? Is he really an environmentalist? Or just connected to Councillors?'

The Secretary barked a laugh. 'Environmentalist! No, no, no such thing. But, yes, he is connected to one of the Councillors. And that is much worse.'

'But we're connected too. To the CS. And to you,' I pointed out boldly.

'Me? Ah, no, no, no. I cannot be of any help. I am not going to pull any case out of its normal procedures. Whatever the procedure for stay orders, you will have to follow that.'

'And the CS?'

'CS? Ah hahaha. No CS can do anything. Annnnything. Not inside the Corporation. That is my jurisdiction only.'

Silently, we filled in the forms required by people facing stay orders and handed them in. The woman at the desk looked sympathetic and, luckily, didn't speak at all. Perhaps she sensed that if she'd uttered even the tiniest platitude, I was ready to soak her shoulder with tears and snot.

After we had filed our application, we drove out to the plot to see if staring at our half-finished house would somehow make us feel better. There it stood. An attractively designed compound wall, an unpainted metal gate, a gigantic half-finished security cabin and a minuscule half-finished house. The inside of the house was a forest of metal scaffolding which had been erected a few days ago in readiness for the roof to be cast. Above our heads were a few planks of wood held up by the scaffolding but mostly there was just blue sky.

The phone rang. It was Builder 2.

'Any luck with the Corporation?' he asked.

'No. Doesn't look good,' I replied.

'Did you get any idea of how long it will take through the normal channels?'

I didn't think he'd understand if I asked, 'How long is a piece of string?' So I merely said, 'Vacating a stay order could take a long time. Like, weeks or months even.'

'I just erected the metal poles for the roof,' he said.

'I know. I can see. I'm at the plot right now.'

'Should I take them down?'

'No!' I said. I wasn't going to give Mr 'Environmentalist' that satisfaction. Nor Builder 1 (who was probably his best friend), for whom no sight would be more satisfying than our construction materials being carted away.

'The scaffolding has all been hired,' Builder 2 reminded me. 'And, with the monsoons coming, they will get rusty and probably ruined. It could cost a lot of money.'

'Can you not do anything to keep them from getting rusty?'

'Well, I could oil them. You get a kind of lubricant meant for metal.' He sounded reluctant, but I leapt at the idea.

'Please. Please do that,' I said. 'And just give me a few days to think of what to do next.'

14

IN THE EVENTLESS DAYS THAT FOLLOWED, MR M AND I, stuck in my mother's 15ft x 15ft guest annexe and sharing a bathroom, had started to get distinctly less keen on each other's company. It didn't help that we were dependent on my mother's kitchen and maid. And it certainly didn't help that Maid was the hands-down winner of World's Worst Maid, having been re-awarded the trophy every year without contest since 1999.

My mother had pretty much rescued Maid from the bylanes of Trivandrum eighteen years ago, helping her to get rid of an alcoholic and abusive husband. She had gone on to educate

Maid's two children and also built the family a small house. In return, Maid had grown so loyal she refused point-blank to work anywhere else. Which would have been a good thing, had she not constantly moaned about how much more she could be earning if she had been able to work elsewhere. Blocks of flats were coming up near her house and, if she cleaned in three, she could be earning enormous amounts of money. Besides, all three employers would buy her clothes at Onam and give her food and many other things to take home, so she was badly off in every way, as she constantly reminded us. Despite being told that she was free to go, she stubbornly stayed on although it was hard to work out if the primary factor was loyalty or laziness or just plain old habit. Whenever a new maid was brought in as a temporary measure, Maid was prone to unfriendliness, sulks and even tantrums. In the meantime, being one of Kerala's newly empowered, financially independent women, she wielded her not inconsiderable powers over my ageing mother, getting her to eat whatever she felt like tossing together or, more usually, serving up food three days old which she had excavated from the depths of the fridge and herself refused to eat. Oh, and if cooking wasn't among her gifts, Maid was also somewhat unenthused by cleaning duties, cursorily twitching a broom about the house every other day and very firmly falling into the 'rinser' rather than 'scrubber' camp in the washing-up department. In another life, she would have been a sparkling socialite, for what really took her fancy was wearing her best sari to go down to the local temple when it served free food on the first of every month or spending weekends visiting far-flung relatives or attending this wedding or that house-warming. She had an amazingly active social circle that seemed to be partying all the time and, when she was stuck at my mother's house, she made up for the boredom by catching up on neighbourhood gossip with the woman who lived next door.

Even though both Mr M and I enjoy cooking occasionally, my mother's kitchen was definitely Maid's territory. Apart from having to duck around her redoubtable presence, any cooking ventures involved a great deal of pre-cleaning in order to bring the kitchen up to our own health and safety standards. Honestly, it was easier to eat whatever Maid knocked up every three days. I also neglected to say earlier that most foods in the house were cooked to an unrecognisable pulp because of Mother's dental issues.

So there we were, seemingly trapped forever in my mother's guest annexe, eating the geriatric food her kitchen turned out, chafing against the poor choices available to us by way of supermarkets and restaurants while the house we had started to build was stuck in the shape of a hollow shell.

Mr M quoted Nietsche for the zillionth time. 'What doesn't kill me makes me stronger.'

'Yeah, yeah, yeah,' I snapped in the privacy of my head.

But God, sitting in his heavenly abode, stroked his beard and, instead of finally casting a kindly sunbeam on us, sent one of his fallen angels to disprove both Mr M and Nietsche in one fell swoop.

15

IT HAPPENED ONE NIGHT AS WE HAD FINISHED dinner and were going down a set of darkened stairs back to our annexe. Mr M, who was a couple of steps ahead of me, staggered and seemed to take a tumble down what was left of the stairs. That's odd, I remembered thinking, as it was one of those rare nights when he had not sneaked in a quick bottle of beer before dinner. Before I could ask, however, I heard him emit a strangled yell and say, 'Light, light!'

I switched the nearest lights on and saw him pointing to a corner of the car porch. In the half-darkness, I could see a small black creature wriggling as though in its death throes. It was, as it happens, in its death throes, but I wasn't that familiar with death throes and, to be honest, it would have been hard to care very much given that it was a ... 'SNAKE!!' I hollered.

'Is it? Is it? You're sure?'

'Well, what do you think? Of course it's a bloody snake!'

'It's a bit small.'

'Well, that still makes it a bloody snake! Did it bite you?'

'I don't know. I felt something.'

'Felt what? What do you mean *something*? Surely you'd know if a snake had bitten you!'

'Well, I felt it wriggle over my foot. That's why I stamped and fell. But I don't know if it bit me or not.'

We stopped yelling at each other and bent over to examine his foot, shining torchlight on it with my phone. And there they were, unmistakably, four little puncture marks, side by side, two just below the big toe and two above.

'It's bitten you! Twice!'

'Bugger me. I didn't feel a thing.'

'Can you feel anything now?'

'What do you mean *feel anything*?'

'I don't know, for chrissake, pain or numbness or stinging of some sort ... it is a bloody snake bite after all!' (Pardon me, but I've always found it curiously soothing to pepper my conversation liberally with the word 'bloody' in moments of crisis.)

Mr M gave me a wild-eyed look before shaking his head and glancing around. 'Where the fuck has it gone?'

We looked at where the snake had last been seen wriggling but in those few seconds it was gone. Vamoose. Thin air. As far as acting skills went, it had put on an Oscar-winning performance of death throes before using the first chance to swiftly disappear. We looked under the car, we looked outside the gate, but it could have been miles away by now. I've read that some of these creatures can travel as fast as seven miles per hour. But right now there was more important stuff to attend to.

We ran back up the stairs and frantically rang my mother's doorbell. Once we'd left for the night, Mother tended to lock up rather zealously, using two sets of keys and three bolts. So we stood in the darkness, listening to her jangling, grinding efforts to open her front door again.

'Fort Bloody Knox,' muttered Mr M, still firing on all four cylinders even though the snake venom was probably coursing energetically through his arteries. I peered at him, trying to make out in the dark if he might be turning blue or grey or whatever colouring poisoned people take on.

To her credit, Mother did not faint or scream or do all the things I'd have expected from someone so terrified of snakes. Instead, she did what she has always done when faced with a crisis: she called her long-suffering younger brother who lives next door.

Uncle was summoned on the telephone and then Mother, stunned into a strange cool-headedness, sat down to tie a tourniquet around Mr M's shin. Once this was done, we left Mother and Aunt clinging to each other in terror at home while the three of us piled into the car, Uncle at the wheel, while I kept up a ceaseless line of chatter to ensure Mr M didn't slip away into unconsciousness. I wasn't very sure if snake bite victims did indeed slip into unconsciousness, but ceaseless chatter seemed worth the effort since there was little else I could do. If nothing else, chattering would keep Uncle awake as he'd almost certainly had his customary three tots before dinner and Mother must have pulled him out of deepest slumber to do this mad midnight run to the hospital.

At the A&E department of the hospital that was nearest to the house, we were told that the only place in Trivandrum that dealt with snake bites was Trivandrum Medical College at the other end of town.

So off we went again, as fast as Uncle's little Santro would carry us, ploughing through the dark, hot Kerala night. Mr M kept answering 'I think so' in an uncharacteristically uncertain manner every time he was asked if he was feeling okay. Which was about every five minutes by either Uncle or me. Mercifully there wasn't much traffic about and, for the first time, I was immensely grateful for Trivandrum's non-existent nightlife.

It was a little after 11 p.m., and a whole hour after the snake's fangs had descended into Mr M's foot, when we finally pulled up outside TMC's A&E department. That's if you can imagine an ancient crumbling building dating back to British times as a proper 'hospital'. Unsurprisingly it was teeming with people, even at that time of night (so that's where Trivandrumwallahs all went to when they deserted the streets), given that this was where anyone who couldn't afford a private hospital went for all manner of ailments.

The man to whom we babbled our confused narrative regarding snakes and steps was unperturbed. 'I will admit you. But have you brought the snake?' he asked.

'The snake gets admitted too?' I responded, confused.

Perhaps it was those three tots, but my normally mild-mannered uncle was suddenly incensed. 'This is nonsense! Why do you want to see the snake? Is it proof you need? You can see the bite mark on his foot. What further proof of snake bite do you need? Hurry up and start the treatment. Immediately!'

'Somebody please tell me what's going on,' pleaded Mr M as we were all talking at great speed in Malayalam.

The hospital man sighed. 'People usually kill the snake after a bite. And they bring it in so that we can tell if it is a poisonous type or not.'

'Oh, I seeee. I'm so sorry but ours got away,' I said. Even if our snake had hung around helpfully in the car porch, I'm not sure I would have had whatever it takes to find an implement and then maniacally beat it to death. Oh, and scoop up its corpse and put it into a receptacle and carry it all the way to the Medical College next to me in the car. I mean, it could have gotten a second wind and revived itself to turn on all the occupants trapped in the car like that *Anaconda* trailer I'd seen through my fingers at the cinema once.

'But you can see he's been bitten,' I said. 'Why don't we just assume it was a poisonous snake and start the treatment without further delay? Do you have antidote for snake venom?' My medical knowledge petered out at that point.

Luckily, the medic had the patience of Job. 'Yes, yes, we will admit him immediately. But we don't administer snake antidote until we are sure. He needs to stay overnight for checking, so you can fill in these forms now.'

I was impressed that Kerala's bureaucracy

had forms for everything, even snake bites, and so I found a place to sit and fill them in while Mr M was taken into an adjoining room for the initial round of tests, Uncle accompanying him as interpreter.

As we were being herded into the general ward, there was a commotion at the entrance; a small group entered, a large man at its head holding a big sack by the neck.

'Snake bite, snake bite,' people said, clearing a path as the group was ushered in. I wondered if the crowd was scattering in all directions due to the speed with which snake venom was known to act or out of fear that whatever was in the sack would free itself and come after them. I was poised for flight myself.

These snakebite victims clearly had prior knowledge of the requirements as, unlike us, they'd had the nous to bring their snake, duly murdered, with them. The sack was opened to reveal its contents to anyone who dared evince interest and Mr M joined the goggling crowd while I politely declined.

Within minutes, Mr M hurried back, hobbling on his tourniqueted leg. 'Bloody hell,' he said, eyes wide. 'You ought to take a gander at that. It's fucking *enormous*! I think it's a python. At least five kilograms in weight.' And, as if that wasn't already too much information, he added in a reverential tone, 'Plus it died with a dead rat clamped in its jaws.'

Just as I was contemplating my options between retching and fainting, we were all—the two Snakebite Parties—corralled into the general ward. Two adjoining beds were found by turfing out relatively well-looking patients and sending them to sleep on the floor. The Other Snakebite Party were terribly smart at this game as they'd also had the uncommon good sense to carry a bedcover with them. I imagined the cool efficiency with which they had rescued their relative from the jaws of a python, before proceeding to kill it and parcel it up for its journey to the hospital while also rifling through their linen cabinet to pick the right bedcover to bring with them. They now laid a sparkling clean cover over the bed they had been assigned.

I gazed at the bed meant for us. It had a sheet on it that had probably never been anywhere near a soap sud in two years. I thought of the many disease-carrying bacteria that would by now have taken up residence amongst its fibres. I would have had difficulty standing on it in boot-shod feet, leave alone trying to spend a night curled up at one end of it. A man from the Other Snakebite Party saw the expression on my face and asked me if I wanted him to buy me a sheet as he was stepping out of the hospital to get some food. The one thing I *had* had the nous to carry with me was my mother's purse and so I handed over a 500-rupee note with a grateful smile.

Within thirty minutes we were all seated on beds, swapping snakebite stories. On the hour, a pair of nurses would come by, take Mr M's pulse and check his breathing. The Medical College staff were serious and business-like and I was terribly impressed by their stoic professionalism, given the army of patients they needed to tend to.

Both Mr M and the fourteen-year-old boy who was the snakebite victim in the Other Party looked in fine fettle, so confidence was growing within me that venom was probably not rushing to their heart and lungs, though there was always the possibility of a slow-acting type ...

Sometime in the middle of the night, we were considered well enough to move off the beds and make way for new patients who were being admitted in a steady stream. As there was nowhere to sit, and I did not feel like joining the legions who were fast asleep under the beds, the Other Snakebite Victim's mother budged up and gave us half a bed to squeeze ourselves into. And there we sat, united in fear and anxiety and general anti-snake sentiment.

It must have been the first time in months that I had not spent a night thinking about my half-finished house by the sea.

Early the next morning, mad with sleep deprivation, Mr M decided he was going to discharge himself without waiting for the obligatory twenty-four hour observation period. 'I promise I won't keel over and die now,' he said and, looking at him, it did seem unlikely that the Grim Reaper was going to whisk him away. He had probably got lucky in attracting a non-poisonous, albeit step-climbing, snake. Besides, we were probably far more in danger of picking up some serious contagion here in this ward. And so we bid goodbye to the Other Snakebite Party, who were also looking, I am pleased to say, exceedingly well. And then we went home.

By the time we got back, tales of Mr M's derring-do had spread around the neighbourhood and all morning we had visitors popping in to exclaim over our bravery and good fortune. It was as I was seeing off the fourth set of visitors at the gate that I stopped to peer more closely at a drainpipe in the corner of the car porch that appeared to have a metal hook behind it. I bent to examine the dull sheen of the metal, wondering why there was a hook in that position, and leapt back about three feet because, on closer examination, the metal hook displayed an unusual scaly surface. It could have been my fervid imagination or maybe a kind of Post Traumatic Stress Syndrome reliving-the-experience thing, but I was taking no chances. I yelled out to the electrician who was doing some work in Mother's house and was leaving on his motorcycle to buy some supplies.

'Please come here and tell me if this looks like a snake to you,' I said, pointing to the bent drainpipe.

The response I got to my question was a high-pitched squeal from somewhere far away.

'Snake! Snake!' was the cry of the electrician, who had abandoned his bike to disappear at a rapid run down the road.

That was all the invitation I needed to bounce at great speed back up the stairs into Mother's house. Mr M was summoned again and returned down the stairs with a motley posse of supporters from the surrounding houses, each of them carrying rods and sticks. After a bit of yelling, in which it was confirmed that the snake was already dead, some brave soul lifted the corpse out using a curtain rod. There the poor creature dangled at the end of the rod, murdered by Mr M's giant foot that had descended on it while it was peacefully making its way up the stairs. After receiving a killer blow of eighty-nine kilos which, to its credit, it had tried to stave off with a double bite, it must have dragged itself, broken bones and all, into the darkest corner it could find in order to curl up and die. You had to feel sorry for it. Especially seeing that Mr M continues to dine out on the story of how he was bitten by a python in the tropical wilds of Kerala but managed to kick it to death with his bare feet.

16

THERE WERE ALONG THE WAY A FEW MORE THRILLS offered up by reptiles—one long, fat, yellow-brown rat-snake uncoiled itself unhurriedly from outside the front door one afternoon as we returned to our room and slid slowly over the tiles before disappearing into the garden. Another (again, an impressively long but essentially harmless rat-snake) came pelting down a slope in my direction as I walked with a friend in the Raj Bhavan gardens. It seemed to be in a state of some distress, raising itself high in intermittent efforts to scale the wall next to it but falling back down again to slither frantically closer and closer towards us. Luckily, it ignored my friend and I as we stood frozen, clutching each other in fright, making a speedy journey past us in the direction of a guard who, having heard our yells, stood ready with his rather impressive looking rifle raised. No butts or bullets were employed, I am pleased to say, as the guard recognised the snake for a harmless one and stepped aside to allow it on its way through the gate to the dense grove of trees on the other side of the wall.

Mostly, however, our months in the wilderness passed by in a state of extreme ennui. We read a lot, took long afternoon naps and, in the evenings, foraged for food (any food, *please*) that wasn't the locally grown produce of bananas (eaten as fruit when ripe and vegetable when unripe) and a whole host of squashes and gourds that Mr M described as 'hospital patient food'.

Our daily constitutionals took place in the grounds of Tagore Theatre, which provided us with a traffic-free undulating leafy pathway that surrounded the popular venue. Circumnavigating this fifteen times took about an hour, by the end of which one also felt a sensation of pleasant dizziness akin to that provided by (I am told) a few puffs of marijuana. Perhaps it was to avoid the dizziness, but I noticed that some of our fellow walkers did every alternate round walking backwards. Given that the path was littered with pebbles and fallen twigs, this seemed like a risky enterprise, but I never saw anyone falling over, alas. This was especially remarkable as Tagore Theatre was, in the years of our perambulations, undergoing a major revamp and the pathway was inevitably impeded by stacks of bricks or rolls of drainpipes or even, for a few weeks, a pair of giant generators that blocked access completely.

Still, all this provided our lives with occasional doses of excitement without which we may well have gone a little mad. There are good reasons why most people leave the parental home while in their teens or twenties and NEVER come back. Certainly not in middle age, by which time one is usually oneself a parent and rather resistant to the business of being parented. I tried to catch myself before snapping at Mother, in whose mind I seemed to have frozen as a permanent six year old.

As a distraction, I occasionally took Mother to her medical appointments. Being the widow of an Air Force officer allowed her limitless free consultations at the military medical services in the Army base at Pangode. A fabulous entitlement, we all agreed, except that it encouraged Mother to take full advantage of the 'limitless' offer and visit the doctor far more often than was strictly necessary.

She got dressed up for these occasions, pulling out one of her starched cotton saris and carefully matching a blouse to it. We were distantly related to the manager of the clinic, a retired Army man, polished and gentlemanly, who made it a point to escort Mother all the way past the waiting, glowering queue right into the doctor's room. This was the practice even if another patient was already being treated and, often, we stood there watching them have their temperature and blood pressure taken, listening to intimate details of ailments that they probably hesitated to tell their spouses.

The doctors themselves were beyond kind to my mother and listened carefully to her complaints, health-related and otherwise. Sometimes they jollied her along, but she didn't seem to mind being treated like a girl, giggling at the chivvying. There was one doctor she particularly favoured, complaining that the other one was 'too old' but, really, she was happy to have any one of them hold her hand and listen to her chest. She could hardly bear to tear herself away from them at the end of the consultation, settling down to polite chit-chat about their own health and asking after their families while I tugged at her elbow, mindful of all those patients still waiting in the queue we'd so rudely jumped.

As we made our way out, some people muttered a bit on seeing my apologetic face but no one ever said anything because Mother ticked three out of three boxes of great importance in Kerala—she was elderly, the widow of a senior officer and, perhaps most crucially, she was being treated like a VIP so chances were that she *was* a VIP. When we had collected the (also free) supplements and medicines, Mother left the clinic happily clutching her brown paper bag like it was a return gift from a child's birthday party.

From my visits to the ECHS clinic, it was apparent that Kerala's biggest health problem at the moment was not born of any disease-carrying germ but, quite simply, obesity. Within a mere twenty years (the length of time I had lived away from Kerala), the shape of the average Malayali had evolved from demure and slight to anything from pleasantly plump to gargantuan. The issue seemed particularly marked amongst women and I couldn't help wondering if it had been created at least partially by feminism. As more and more women joined the workplace and became financially empowered, most households were no longer able to turn out the traditional, labour-intensive, low-fat foods that Kerala specialised in—all those delicious thorans and avials that needed no more than a teaspoon of fat to cook but required time to prepare because of having to grate and grind the ubiquitous coconut, now declared a superfood by the international health industry. Easier by far for the hard-pressed working woman to collect a pack of ready-made biriyani or beef fry from one of the fast-food vans that lined the roads in the evening hours with the express intention of tempting customers on their way home from office.

But what would I rather have? My Malayali sisters now a tad weightier but out-and-about earning their own bread (literally) or stuck at home, painstakingly turning out dosas at breakfast as their mothers and grandmothers had done for years? There was no contest really. I stood firmly, well-padded shoulder-to-shoulder, with them.

Mother went to the HSBC bank expressly to meet one such empowered female who had redefined the standards of professionalism. Unlike the State Bank which Mother was forced to use in order to collect her Air Force widow's pension, the service at HSBC was full of private-sector solicitousness and the pretty lady who dealt with Mother kept sweets rather than dusty paper clips in a bowl on her desk. Mother was ushered into her plush air-conditioned offices by a uniformed guard and seated in a comfortably upholstered chair at a desk from where she was never asked to get up and go to another counter. Instead, the female officer, recognising perhaps instinctively what good customer service should be about, always summoned the requisite person from behind their counter with instructions to bring before Mother whatever paper needed signing or money that was being paid in or withdrawn. Mother went to this bank with the air of a woman going into a beauty parlour, in the mood for a bit of cossetting and pampering. I suppose it was cheaper, and took less time than beauty parlours would have done. And all it had taken was the presence of a female manager to achieve this.

As to whether Mother was enjoying having us installed in her house as seemingly permanent house-guests, the honest answer would be, 'I don't know'. Everyone else thought it was wonderful for her, cooing about how lucky she was to have us 'settling' in Kerala just as she was starting to get old. And, of course, I like to think that we enhanced my mother's life by providing high-class conversation at the dining table and doing most of the household shopping or making her a cup of tea in the afternoon. Occasionally she agreed to a meal out with us (only if it was somewhere cheap and vegetarian) or to a Malayalam movie (which she really enjoyed, especially if it starred Mohanlal, her old classmate's son) so I suppose we provided some entertainment too. But, all said and done, I can't help thinking we weren't the best company for someone approaching her eighties.

For one, construction woes overwhelmed most of our high-class conversations. Then there were all my territorial battles with Maid and, although Mother complained about her too, I got the distinct impression that, in the event of a serious falling-out and parting of ways, Mother would actually find it easier to do without me than Maid. Over their years of enforced togetherness, they had become almost like an old married couple and I was sure it would take a crowbar to separate them, much as they hated each other on most days.

17

THROUGH ALL THAT TIME, THE MONSOONS CAME AND went and I tried to comfort myself that work on the house would have stopped anyway during such an unrelenting deluge. Once in a while, however, we felt compelled to drive out to Veli and gaze forlornly at our roofless, half-built house, trying to imagine what it would have looked like with a ceiling and a terrace and a front door. I imagined living in it, cooking, bathing, eating, sleeping, all those things people do every day in their houses all over the world without having to clear immovable stay orders imposed by their local Corporation. Returning to London wasn't possible either, since our house had just been rented for another year. We were well and truly stuck.

Was there anything that could have made things worse? Ah, yes. There was a KSRTC bus.

The public buses run by the Kerala State Road Transport Corporation are like large dented tin cans that careen around narrow roads with little regard for other vehicles or pedestrians. They were nothing like London's red Routemasters that trundled along obediently in their bus lanes, lowering themselves with a little sigh of their hydraulic suspension to pick up the elderly or disabled. These KSRTC buses were killing machines driven predominantly by muscular young men with heaps of bad attitude, and we were about to discover how bad this attitude really was. Every day the papers carried at least one piece of news about a child or a scooterist knocked over by a KSRTC bus and Mr M and I had both learnt to respectfully give way to these vehicular behemoths while driving, swerving and bouncing into ditches in order to make room if a bus was oncoming.

This particular one wasn't oncoming but stuck behind us in the commuter rush as we returned to town from Veli one evening. The five-kilometre distance from the airport to the General Hospital was obviously too long a time to be stuck behind a boring grey VW Polo and the driver of the bus, impatient with the dullness of the backs of our heads, had started to flash his lights and blare his horn in longer and louder intervals. The sensible thing to do was to give way (the alternative being to go faster and faster and possibly mow down a hapless pedestrian or two in the process). But Mr M clearly wasn't feeling very sensible and jutted his chin, refusing to pull over. I looked over my shoulder nervously and saw the truly terrifying sight of a crazily swaying bus, seemingly inches away from our rear windscreen, the driver mouthing angrily (he was near enough for me to discern what he was mouthing: it was not polite) and waving one free hand (not in a friendly way) and continuing to toot his horn (also not in a hello-there way, but by now you will have got the picture).

Perhaps encouraged by my rabbit-in-headlights look, the bus driver suddenly proceeded to swing his vehicle to the left in order to overtake us from the wrong side. He had either failed to see the roadworks on that side or was feeling macho enough to fly right over them in James Bond style but, in the next few seconds, he was tearing into the side of our vehicle with the side of his bus. I heard a long, nasty scrunching sound as, having finished trying to rob me of my left shoulder, the bumper of the bus locked with ours and wrenched a part of it out to drag along the road. Sparks flew and, cleaved to each other thus, bumper to bumper, we all screeched to an undignified halt. Of course, people gathered immediately and all the bus passengers disembarked and started shouting at us (this inconsiderate disruption to their day could only have been our fault seeing that we were rich people sitting in a car). Emboldened by the socialist support, the bus driver and conductor also started shouting but, while Mr M took photos of the accident on his phone, I made a swift call to our old friend CS, who called his old friend the IG of Police, who promised to call his old friend who was in charge of Road Traffic Accidents and, within minutes, a police jeep was with us. We were towed to the police station in Pattom that dealt with Trivandrum's accidents and, as happens in India, the network of 'contacts' that swung into action ensured we were greeted as we arrived at the police station like long-lost friends.

In the room of a senior policeman we were offered tea, which was surely not a beverage on offer to all those other RTA victims thronging the corridor and I knew we ought to consider ourselves lucky. However, the policeman's advice startled us.

'Let me say this. You should not even consider a case against the KSRTC driver,' he warned. 'You see, they have such a strong union, nobody can touch them.'

'Not even you?' Mr M asked.

The policeman shook his head sadly. 'Not even the police. They will come and start stoning the station by evening if we allow you to register a case.'

I was incredulous. 'Well then, is it any wonder they drive like maniacs? They can kill as many people as they like, safe in the knowledge that the police will never take any action against them!'

The policeman looked a little sheepish, but he remained silent and it was amply clear that he did not want us to file a case against the KSRTC. Not on his watch at any rate.

'We need to discuss this in private,' Mr M said to me.

Outside in the corridor, he asked me if it was possible that the police were hand in glove with the KSRTC union.

'Not sure, but of course it's possible,' I replied. 'It would explain his advice to us.'

'We don't need to take his advice,' Mr M said.

'But what he says about the unions in Kerala is true ...'

We were interrupted at this point by a man who introduced himself to us as a KSRTC trainer. Trailing after him were the errant bus driver and conductor whose demeanour had by now transformed from the aggressiveness of our roadside encounter into one of abject apology. They had worked out that we were people with 'influence' and, regardless of the power wielded by their union, they were rattled.

'He is very sorry,' the KSRTC representative said, waving in the direction of the driver. 'He has two small children and does not want to lose his job.' In the background, at the mention of his children, the driver swiftly hung his head and tried to look both abject and fatherly.

'Well, maybe he should be considering the children of all those motorists he shows such little regard for when he drives his bus.'

Mr M cut in. 'You said you're a trainer. Have you told him that what he drives is a bus, not a weapon?'

The bus driver darted forward and grabbed Mr M's hand. 'Sorry sir. Sorry sir. I should not have driven like that, sir. I should not have got angry, sir. Sir, please forgive. Please forgive.' Mr M knew little Malayalam but, from all that sirring, he could surely work out it was an apology.

The scene was causing heads to turn and Mr M, extricating himself from the driver's grip, said to me, 'Let's get out of here. I don't think I can stand any more of this.'

We popped back into the office of the policeman to tell him we had decided not to pursue a case against the bus driver. He looked visibly relieved. 'Good decision,' he said. 'A case gets nobody anywhere as it just drags on for years. Who has the time these days for such nonsense, eh?'

18

HALF-HEARTED EFFORTS TO VACATE THE STAY ORDER continued apace and then, one balmy evening, we hit an unexpected jackpot. The idea came from CS, who—in a bid to cheer us up after our brush with the bus—had invited us to the Taj Kovalam's lovely seaside restaurant for dinner.

It was easy to forget our little problems while sitting under the palms and listening to the rustling of the sea breeze among their fronds. The ocean was a glinting blackness lapping gently a few feet away and, in the distance, squid-catchers strung their lights along the horizon as though illuminating it for our pleasure. Kerala is truly a paradise at moments like this.

Tucking into a giant slab of grilled tuna, CS said, 'I was thinking about your Veli project ... since the CRZ is supposedly the biggest stumbling block, maybe we should go straight to the CRZ people. And then work our way down from there.'

'But who are the CRZ people? I thought it was just a piece of legislation.'

'Well, there's a panel that examines all plans put forward by the Corporation which have any bearing on the CRZ. It's a small panel but the Chairman is effectively it. He's a scientist, with a vast knowledge of the ecology of the coastline so everyone else on the panel kowtows to him. Dr R. Nice guy,' our friend said.

'You *know* him?' I asked, my pulse quickening. We will all accept by now what an important question that is in India.

'Hmmm ... we've worked together on a few projects,' CS said modestly. But I sensed we were on the verge of a breakthrough.

The following day, a phone call was made, an appointment sought and, within a day or two, we were in the offices of Dr R, Mr CRZ. He didn't look like a scientist, wearing normal clothes, not a lab coat with pipettes sticking out of its pockets as I'd vaguely imagined. He also behaved like a normal person, listening to our rather garbled story about builders and social activists and stay orders with indignantly twitching bushy eyebrows.

'Someone is harassing you unnecessarily,' he said. 'Veli is a built-up area and has been so for a number of years. There are no building restrictions there except for the usual Corporation rules. In fact, the locals are always building on *poramboke* land, closer and closer to the sea, and yet nobody ever stops them. Where else can they build after all but on the High Tide Line if they can afford nothing else? We recognise they need to be near the sea to carry out their trade. So there are hardly any regulations in that area anyway. I see no reason why you cannot build your house on legitimately purchased land.'

It took all my self-control to stop from leaping out of my seat to shower this dear man's face with kisses.

'How do we get construction restarted, sir? We can't just ignore the stay order, can we?' Mr M asked.

'Well, let's start by my visiting your site. I will do a report and send my findings to the Corporation. It might be easier to raise a fresh planning application rather than applying to clear the stay order on the old one. Let me think about that.' (When a clever Malayali tells me he is thinking, I know enough to retire silently.)

As good as his word, Dr R came to our plot a few days later along with a colleague—another startlingly unscientist-like figure—the two of them fetching up cheerily on a motorcycle. Having looked at the plot, they visited the neighbour's house (him of the cutlass incident) and got his Corporation door number. The CRZ, that great big mystical onion which revealed new and fascinating layers every time I discussed it, apparently stipulated that special permission was not required for any construction that had another legitimate building located between it and the sea. Since Neighbour's house lay a few feet closer to the sea than our structure, we were safe and dry, so to speak.

With these comforting words, Dr R roared off on the pillion of his friend's motorcycle. Two angels on an unlikely chariot.

Forget angels. It was like having been given special dispensation by God himself. Nobody in the planning department of Trivandrum Corporation could seem to believe that our new application had been passed by the remote and transcendent CRZ authority. The blue CRZ stamp on our document got a lot of disbelieving, peering looks as it was passed from desk to desk. One Corporation bod even turned the document over as though expecting the reverse side to hold a rational explanation for this total travesty. Then he looked up at us open-mouthed and, I suspect, just a little bit incensed at having been denied his rightful share of palm-grease. But, glory be, that CRZ stamp was all it took in the end to have our new application sent swiftly onwards and upwards through those labyrinthine and perilous corridors of power.

Once all the permissions were in place, we returned to the office of Architect 2 like triumphant warriors and, to great whoops of delight, Builder 2 was summoned and instructed to restart our construction.

It was another rush to cast the roof and complete the outer structure by the next monsoon, but this time we did it.

Every year in the sweltering heat of May, the newspapers keep people going by providing inch-by-inch news of the progress of the south-west monsoon accompanied by grainy satellite photos that are indecipherable to anyone but a senior meteorologist. Predicting its arrival is an annual game that everyone in Kerala seems to love playing, especially catching each other out when the deluge breaks over the unsuspecting heads of schoolchildren and office-goers.

One particularly still and dark evening in early June, I used the bamboo scaffolding that was still in place to clamber onto our newly cast roof and look at the southern skies. What I beheld was a sight so dramatic, I doubt I will witness anything like it ever again. The sea was silver close to the coast, lapping calmly and innocently, as if totally unaware that, in the far distance, its waters had turned a deep, livid grey-black. Above it were clouds whose ilk I had never seen before. These were not the soft white scudding things that float around in England's skies with seemingly no other intention than to delight the hearts of Messrs Wordsworth and Keats. Weighing down the horizon here were colossal dark vapour structures, churning and roiling like a wrathful giant awakened too early from his sleep. This outraged ogre was now taking slow, plodding steps in our direction and the little girl in me, responding to the fear centre in her amygdala, wanted to run as fast as she could in the opposite direction. Of course, I'd seen the monsoons many times during my childhood holidays in Kerala but those experiences involved no more than pressing my nose against soaking wet window-panes or spending afternoons curled up under a blanket while listening to the drumming of rain on the roof-tiles of my grandmother's house.

This vision had me scuttling back downstairs to safety. Good thing too, for, when the monsoon finally broke over the Veli coast an hour later, it came in horizontal sheets. What was pelting the parched earth was not ordinary rain but water-bullets pocking the sand. Within minutes, it had virtually drowned all our plants and seemed to be doing a pretty good job of trying to bring down all our trees too. And the howling! That irate giant was much, much angrier than I'd first thought.

19

THE MONSOONS PROVIDE ONE GOOD REASON, BUT the truth is that Kerala really needs little excuse to down tools and stop work. Strikes and processions are commonplace and Trivandrum, being the capital, is festooned with red flags (sometimes yellow or blue, depending on which political party has called the strike) which gives the town the falsely jolly air of a birthday party.

The state has remained reassuringly non-communal so far but this could be changing—rather alarmingly—as political parties begin wooing this religious or that caste group in order to shore up their own numbers. This game makes for bewildering bedfellows too and enormous posters of what resemble rogues' galleries commandeer walls and loom over pavements. When a national leader visits, the rogues' galleries shuffle up to accommodate their picture as well and so Narendra Modi or Sonia Gandhi are often cheek by jowl with some moustachioed, khadi-clad Kerala politico they surely have no desire at all to meet in real life.

One such poster had become the bane of my existence as it was about ten feet high and six feet wide and straddled the pavement that led from my mother's house to the Milma booth from where I often bought milk and the newspapers after a morning walk. Whoever put it there had assumed that all pavement walkers were of Lilliputian dimension for there was no more than a three-foot gap between the bottom of the poster and the top of the pavement so, walking along, one was faced with the choice of either limbo dancing one's way under this picture of a leering politician, or stepping off the pavement into the face of sure death.

Trivandrum's pavements, in fact, operated like deathtraps in many ingenious ways and a dreamy morning walker could end up dramatically spreadeagled at the bottom of an open manhole or suddenly dead by swift garrotting if a new poster had been erected overnight and its supporting ropes had been tied to a lamp post or tree right across the path. An innocent early riser or temple-goer could never imagine the army of elves that were out at night plotting their destruction in this way.

The problem really was that nobody expected people to be foolish enough to walk. Why on earth would you walk anywhere if you could afford a set of wheels? In prosperous Kerala, most people could afford at least a two-wheeler and even the poorest used the KSRTC buses. Even those with a fondness for exercise generally got into their cars or mounted their scooters all gung-ho and drove at breakneck speed to Tagore Gardens or the Museum grounds to join the human carousel.

I often did the museum merry-go-round myself, except I liked to walk to the grounds as it was only ten minutes away from where my mother lived. This, however, involved crossing the Vellayambalam roundabout which, I had found, was the most effective deathtrap provided by Trivandrum if one was feeling particularly daring. Vehicles approached this roundabout with the zeal of a hara-kiri mission and screeched to a halt with barely disguised resentment if caught out by a red light. It wasn't as though pedestrian crossings had not been provided, and a little green man even lit up when traffic going straight halted for the red. However, nobody had told the people turning left that there was a pavement-treading species that enjoyed certain rights too. Not that I ever crossed with an air of entitlement, of course. It was much more a mad dash at my nimble best to the safety of the far pavement.

Nevertheless, this felony caused me to be at the receiving end of slammed brakes, dark glares and dirty looks and even, on one occasion, a shaken fist that had a finger pointing heavenwards which is where I was grateful not to have been despatched prematurely.

Once, when it all became too much for me to handle, I marched across to the policeman on whose unfortunate beat Vellayambalam roundabout fell that day. He looked about fifteen, but he wore his uniform with an air of authority.

'Can you not see, I have been trying to cross this road for the last ten minutes,' I said—or rather screeched, as I needed to make myself audible over the evening traffic. 'But nobody stops, even when I get my light. Somebody needs to tell these people that a left turn isn't a free turn!'

'Madam,' the policeman replied, now wearing the fatigued air of a seventy-year-old, 'we have been trying to tell these people that they have to wait for the left filter light but nobody listens!'

'If they won't listen to you in your uniform, then what hope is there for the rest of us?' I asked in horror.

Now he looked close to tears himself, and back to being fifteen. His voice was a wail. 'What to do, Madam. Public are not scared of my uniform. They simply ignore me. It is the culture of this place.'

We could have sobbed our collective frustration out on each other's shoulders, this young policeman barely out of school whom no one would listen to, even when he wore his uniform, and I, a frustrated resident of this city. But we chose the path of dignity, nodded in mutual recognition of being misfits in an unsympathetic and uncultured world and parted ways.

20

THE FAST-CHANGING CULTURE OF KERALA WAS clearly exercising the police force in more ways than one. When we went to supervise the construction, we found that the beach was a magnet for young, illicit love, especially in the hot afternoon sun when no one else came to the beach and college lectures were at their most boring. They sat there, under brightly coloured umbrellas, motorcycle helmets flung on the sand, holding hands and canoodling and doing all the things young lovers do with such rash hope. What these hapless folk did not know was that the Vettukaud police liked nothing better than to round up young lovers and haul them off to the police station for a good ticking off. I had seen a few such youngsters sitting wide-eyed with fear in the back of a police jeep, and was tempted to halt their progress to ask why the police force was wasting its time when there were murderous motorists to catch (perhaps even murderous murderers) but, alas, I lacked the gumption. I had, after all, only very recently been described as 'law-abiding' by one of their own kind and wasn't in a hurry to disabuse them of this notion.

This is the thing that's so difficult to explain to non-Malayalis. The strong streak of conservatism that overshadows and negates all those statistics that Keralites love bragging about; enviable demographics around education and health and child mortality and women's empowerment that are shared with developed countries. A subtle example of that conservatism emerged in a conversation with a friend who recounted visiting an elderly relative that morning. When she arrived at her aunt's house, she found that the lady had gone for a walk.

'Ah, nice. Does she walk with friends?' my friend asked her uncle.

'Friends!?' the man responded, a touch horrified. 'No, no, no such thing as friends and all such nonsense. Luckily, my wife doesn't waste time that way. I allow her to go for a walk every morning because the exercise is good for her.'

See what I mean by 'subtle conservatism'? So subtle as to be nearly invisible when we're talking about women who enjoy all the obvious trappings of emancipation. Malayali women come across as particularly fortunate when compared to their sisters in other Indian states (the best example being offered by Mr M's home state of Uttar Pradesh) who continue to be severely downtrodden by deep-rooted patriarchy and chauvinism that take much more obvious forms. But stating with pride that a wife has 'no friends' and is 'allowed' to go for a walk every morning? The worst chauvinists are those who do not even recognise their own chauvinism.

Kerala is indubitably a good aberration in modern India and most people are aware that it is the only state to have achieved total literacy many years ago (not an untrue claim, although the measure of literacy is sometimes merely the ability to sign one's name). Most non-Malayalis also have a vague notion about the matrilineal system followed by the state's large Nair community and genuinely believe that Kerala's women are highly educated and empowered beings. Again, this is not untrue. Most women in Kerala, especially the poor, go out to work and proudly bring home their own bacon/beef/fish. The problem, however, is that this veneer of feminism is a double-edged and very sharp sword. Perhaps its history does go all the way back to the matrilineal system, but the very act of empowering women to own their own homes and earn their own money would appear to have emasculated some men to the extent that they feel little responsibility towards home, hearth and even, sometimes, their own children. Maid's husband was a shining example of that pathetic male species, lurching drunkenly back to her house whenever he was in need of money or medication and raining blows on her if she got mouthy or refused help.

This male apathy extends, unsurprisingly, to unemployment, alcoholism and sometimes results tragically in suicide (few know that Kerala's suicide figures are amongst the highest in India).

An unexpected offshoot of this—in an odd reversal of the Gulf rush—is that the state has become something of a Mecca for large numbers of migrant workers from other states who now flock to Kerala in search of well-paid work. They come from as far away as Bihar and Uttar Pradesh and even Nepal and, at the present time, number an enormous band of

2.5 million people, mostly single men between the ages of 20 and 30. Like migratory birds, their arrival is in times of good weather and rich pickings, specifically during those five months from October to March when the tourist season fills up Kerala's resorts and the demand for exotic food is high.

We soon became frequent day-trippers to Varkala, one such seaside resort just up the coast from us that had a couple of calm blue bays perfect for sea-swimming. In October, we discovered that it was a popular destination for young back-packing Westerners escaping the European winters. As a result, by November, up cropped row upon row of temporary Goa-style shacks along the eating strip on the cliff. Every single one of them was manned by non-Kerala staff and Mr M plunged with great glee into the joy of being able to chat in Hindi, his mother-tongue. I noticed the torrent of words that he had been stocking up behind Malayalam floodgates as he jabbered non-stop that November afternoon. Less than a week later, he was asking, 'When can we go to Varkala again?'

Thanks to those 2.5 million North Indian migrants, he did not have to travel to Varkala every time he wanted to speak Hindi, however. Even our new electrician, a man called Cleatus, turned up with an apprentice in tow who turned out to be from Mr M's state of UP.

'Cleatus? Is that a Malayali name?' Mr M asked, still unfamiliar with the inventiveness of Kerala Christian nomenclature (our neighbours included a 'Bosco', a 'Jijo', a 'Joji', a 'Donaald' and even a rather Asterix-ish 'Scholastica').

'Yes, I am full Malayali,' Cleatus replied.

'But your employee here is from UP.'

'Ah yes, I refuse to employ Malayalis, lazy bastards,' Cleatus explained.

Mr M found this hilarious, naturally, and got chatting animatedly to the pair of them.

'So you communicate with each other in Hindi then?' he asked.

'Well, I learnt Hindi in Goa,' Cleatus replied. 'Worked there many years before coming back here, you see. You worked in London, sir? You are English?'

'No, no, not English. I'm full Indian too. Though not Malayali, alas,' Mr M replied. He then turned to the apprentice, 'And have you learnt any Malayalam?' he asked.

'Him? Malayalam?' Cleatus interjected, thumping his apprentice on the back. 'Is he capable of learning anything, I ask you? He's a UP-wallah, sir. Stupid bastards, the lot of them.'

21

Talking of stupid bastards ...

As mentioned earlier, Kerala's muddled alcohol policy went through a number of baffling changes before getting finally derailed by a change of government. Its latest avatar was, however, totally nobbled by a Supreme Court ruling in 2017, which disallowed any commercial establishment anywhere in the country from selling alcohol if said establishment fell within 500 metres of a highway. Good intentions, but we all know that the road to perdition (or, in this case, highway to hell) is paved with ... etc., etc.

Now, anyone familiar with the narrow

shape of Kerala will know that the state is energetically criss-crossed by several state and national highways. If you spit hard enough, chances are your spittle will fall on a highway of some description. Uncle was particularly devastated to find that his beloved club (Trivandrum Tennis Club) was found to lie on one such highway. Even more gallingly, said highway veered off at a nearby roundabout, turning right rather than going straight as one would reasonably expect, leading to the scandalous outcome that the other two clubs in town (Trivandrum Club and Sri Moolam Club) were not sitting on highways. The iniquitousness of this travesty had reduced many a TTC member to bitter tears, I am reliably informed.

Anyway, overnight, Kerala was back (pretty much) to its dry state, this time by default. This was terrible news for the tourist trade—one of the last successful industries left in the state due to the havoc created by unions. Of the Supreme Court decision, even the Principal Secretary of Tourism used the media to gloomily declare, 'This is the death knell as far as Kerala Tourism is concerned.' Certainly, the numbers would appear to bear this out. Two years after the implementation of the 2014 alcohol ban, foreign tourist arrivals decreased from 7.6 per cent to 6.2 per cent. This might not sound like too devastating a slide until somebody informs you that in 2010 the number had been a glorious 18.3 per cent. In direct consequence, the foreign exchange earnings went from 15 per cent in 2014 to 11.5 per cent in 2016 and is no doubt headed firmly south as I write.

When will our governments realise that bans do not miraculously stop people from indulging in banned substances, merely driving them to carry on their activities underground? A few ingenious ideas swiftly emerged among bar-owners, necessity being the mother of invention and all that. My favourite one came from a roadside hotelier near Ernakulam who, rather than running around squawking in blind panic, calmly set about building a walled labyrinth between the highway and his bar. The papers were full of aerial images of this charming cement construction vaguely reminiscent of the hedge follies of ancient English gardens. It even made it to the pages of *The Guardian*. By creating this labyrinth, the bar-owner had cannily increased the distance from the highway to the door of his establishment to just over 500m. The local police station confirmed that this was perfectly lawful as the ruling did not measure the distance between road and bar as the crow flies but in distance *walked*. (See, that thing again: for every clever law, there will be a cleverer solution floating around somewhere when you're dealing with Malayalis.)

Even if such bans did achieve the happy result of people shunning the amber nectar, a government simply cannot instruct foreign tourists to steer clear of alcohol during the one luxury holiday they have saved up for all year. Kerala, going by the tourism department's own prize-winning advertising campaign, offers a lush green paradise, restful and easy-going, crammed with fresh healthful seafood served aboard converted rice-boats that chug lazily along palm-fringed backwaters. Try asking the average Western tourist to board one such boat on a hot afternoon and fail to stick a chilled and gently sweating bottle of beer in his hand ... I guarantee trouble ahead.

Government bods should remember: tourists are not exactly coming to Kerala for the customer service.

We found that out for ourselves whenever we ate out, increasingly accustomed to being told that this or that was not on the menu. Given the hot climate, the most puzzling of such permanently non-available items was ice as Malayalis seemed strangely unacquainted with small cubes of frozen water that, in

England or America or even in Delhi was brought to your table in massive buckets. Whenever (which was often) Mr M asked for ice in a Kerala watering hole, we were met with expressions on a procession of waiters' faces that ranged from mystified to baffled to downright antagonistic. It had got so bad that the minute Mr M uttered the word 'ice', it triggered a migraine response somewhere deep inside my head.

One evening, a new neighbourhood restaurant took star rating in our numerous experiences of poor customer service. We'd taken a large group of friends and family with us on this occasion. Once we'd settled around a large table in the garden, there rose the question of drinks. We knew there would be no point asking for ice or even for beers as this was, no, not bordering a highway, but merely an unlicensed establishment.

'Do you have Diet Coke?' Mr M asked.

'No, sir,' was the response.

'Diet Pepsi?'

'No, sir, only normal Pepsi.'

'Fresh lime soda?'

'No, sir.'

'Okay, what do you have then?'

'We can get you fresh lime water,' the waiter said decisively.

Mr M was always unwilling to be taken in by assurances of 'filter water'. He decided to push it. 'Well, if you can make fresh lime water, surely you could get a couple of bottles of soda from the shop next door and make fresh lime soda, couldn't you?'

'No, sir. Sorry, sir.'

'Why not?'

I started to shift in my seat, aware that from this point we were a hair's breadth away from storming out, friends, family and all. And we hadn't even gotten around to mentioning the word 'ice'. That familiar old migraine was rearing its head somewhere at the back of my own. I was also keenly conscious that Mother and Aunt, with various pairs of bad knees and ankles between them, were in no position to do very effective storming.

'Your water is filtered, isn't it?' I asked, trying to distract and symbolically using some of said substance to douse the flames that were just about to leap to life. But the waiter, silly man, had no idea I was at this point in time his best decoy.

He ignored me and kept his eyes on Mr M in an admirable effort at being manful. 'Sir, there is no one to go to the shop for soda, sir.'

Mr M's hackles were by now sky-high. 'Okay, how about this? I will go to the shop and use MY money to buy a couple of bottles of soda. Then I will bring them back and YOU can take them to the kitchen and ask them to make us seven fresh lime sodas. Do YOU think you could ask THEM to do that, huh?'

Everyone at the table jumped a little at the shouted use of each pronoun. The waiter, unused to having seven sets of terrified eyes fixed on him, awaiting his response in breathless anticipation, chose the wisest form of least resistance. He backed down, mumbling, 'I will go and check, sir.'

But Mr M was really into his pronouns now. 'Check with WHOM?'

'Manager, sir.'

Mr M was clearly too thirsty to wait for the manager and jumped up to depart for the shop next door. By the time he reappeared carrying two large litre bottles of soda, the manager was at our table, being sweet-talked by various female members of my family. We had managed to soften him considerably for, as soon as Mr M came, he accepted the bottles of soda with a charming smile and promised us our drinks in ten minutes.

Pleased with this small victory, Mr M beamed around the table, accepting the congratulations. At this point Uncle joined us, coming straight from the bar at Trivandrum Tennis Club in a slightly belligerent state. After

Mr M had narrated our experience, he turned to the waiter who was still hovering, notebook and pencil at the ready.

'You don't serve hard drinks?' Uncle demanded.

'No, sir.'

'You don't serve soft drinks,' Uncle continued. Now the hapless waiter took refuge in polite silence. 'Then let me ask you this. WHAT do you serve?'

Aunt patted Uncle's arm and, as is his wont, he swiftly subsided. 'Let's order food,' she said, using her maternal voice, which always worked a treat on him.

'My order is very simple,' Uncle said. 'Fish curry and rice.'

'You have fish curry and rice?' Aunt asked the waiter, though it was only a rhetorical question as there could be few establishments in Kerala that did not serve fish curry and rice.

'We have fish curry, madam. But no rice, sorry, madam. Rice we only make at lunchtime.'

Our friend Rema, probably taking her cue from Mr M, leapt out of her chair. 'Then let me come into the kitchen and make some rice for you,' she said.

Of course, Rema was pressed back into her chair and the restaurant did eventually come up with the goods, serving Uncle a bowl of steaming rice to accompany his fish curry. But the question remains: why does customer service have to be beaten thus out of a Kerala establishment?

I have a long-winded theory about a proud race that has never encountered domination or suffering and, therefore, does not know how to serve and kowtow and gratify. But Mr M has a simpler explanation. Just blame the Commies, he says.

22

AFTER DR R-CRZ-GURU'S INTERVENTION, THE house construction was (to use another nautical expression but joyfully this time) plain sailing. Save for the odd *nokku-kooli* incident, we completed work on what eventually turned into a spacious studio rather than a conventional house due to the floor-area constraints. To compensate for the lack of space, we converted the flat top of the house into a massive terrace covered by a beautiful, old-fashioned terracotta roof. It was a space perfect for gathering people around, especially after we'd lugged our old eight-seater dining table upstairs and tucked a tiny toilet and washbasin next to the water-tanks, the world's tiniest bathroom.

The studio was all cool blue and grey to reflect the sea visible from all the western windows while the terrace was painted in shades of yellow and orange in homage to the heart-stoppingly lovely sunsets we were treated to every evening at exactly half past six.

As it seemed a shame to waste the giant storeroom that had been made by Builder 1 for his pampered cement bags, we converted it into a tiny spare 'bedroom' with its own attached shower. 'Waste not, want not,' Mother said, looking on in satisfaction at what would become her bedroom whenever she was feeling adventurous and fancied a night away from her town house.

And thus we finally moved out of Mother's guest annexe, earning an enthusiastic farewell from Maid. Suddenly awash with space, Mr M and I took (with a delight that we didn't bother masking any more) to spreading ourselves out and putting as many feet between us as we possibly could. Much as we still liked each other, the enforced togetherness of the last couple of years had taken its toll. No more the careful scheduling of morning coffees to ensure we didn't both need the toilet at the same time. No more cries of 'My turn to charge the phone'. No more having to dance around each other just to get from bed to bath. No more zigging when the other zagged (thank you, Alan Bennet).

We hosted a house-warming party and invited all the locals for lunch while my relatives (for whom fishermen were still a scary, alien species) came trepidatiously for dinner, not realising that they were far more likely to meet a bloody end at Vellayambalam roundabout in the heart of town than among the fisher folk of Veli.

Not many of the nokku-kooli brigade accepted our invitation, probably due to the embarrassing fact that many celebratory meals had already been eaten at our expense. Or perhaps they had little desire to witness Mr M gnashing his teeth one more time as that was all they had ever seen of him. But the rest of the neighbourhood came, dressed in their finest, many bearing gifts. They loaded up their plates with parotta and beef fry and, hopefully, a good time was had by all.

The following day, Mrs Cutlass from next door showed her gratitude by handing lunch over the wall (yes, the same wall that had caused all the cutlass-brandishing in what now seemed like another age). Held up by their stiff tails were two gleaming silver mackerel, fresh from the sea and encrusted in salt and sand.

A final word about our fisher folk neighbours. In the two years we spent building (and not building) our house, I watched with a mix of admiration and annoyance the manner in which these proud people stubbornly carried on plying their trade in the face of changing technology and nature's vagaries. Climate change was causing the fishing season to get shorter and less predictable, mechanised trawlers were cutting deep into the waters mined by traditional boats, fish stocks were depleting dramatically and the monsoons were longer and harder than before, which meant that non-fishing periods stretched unsustainably, leading the women to pawn their meagre jewellery in order to make do. It was clear to even a novice like me that this way of life was doomed to disappear, not unlike fishing communities in far more developed countries (an American friend, on hearing my stories of Kerala fishermen, had gifted me Peter Matthiessen's *Men's Lives*, a moving elegy to the now extinct bay men of New England).

I heard from a local union leader about our fishermen's protests against the Meenakumari report, a set of recommendations written up by a Director General of the Central Marine Fisheries Department who, while recommending a trawling ban on native fishing vessels had also, allegedly, allowed foreign boats to fish in India's exclusive economic zone. The trawling ban, normally observed for forty-five days, went back as long as anyone could remember and had always been respected by the fishermen as its primary function was to allow the replenishment of fish stocks during the spawning period. Besides, it kept fishermen safely at home when the ocean was at its most treacherous. In June 2015, however, Kerala's fishermen defied the extended sixty-one day ban and sailed out into the swelling monsoonal sea. It was either that or starvation, said Vijayankutty, the union leader.

Some of our neighbours, in possible recognition of their inescapable eventual fate, had found jobs at the Titanium factory or worked as lifeguards on the beach. Some took employment as sweepers and gardeners at the Tourist Village nearby while their teenage sons came around to shin up our trees and collect tender coconuts to sell to tourists during the season—the healthiest, purest, most eco-friendly drink in the world. Additionally, most of the fisherfolk sent their children to school, hoping, it was clear, to give them a better chance at learning another trade.

Many, however—like Ravindran next door and Vijayan further up the beach—simply carried on fishing, gathering their teams at the crack of dawn to help push the giant wooden boats out to sea with their traditional chants. Inevitably, the boats returned many hours later with near-empty nets but the men, their hard brown bodies dusted with salt, looked energised rather than gloomy. I could not help wondering if it was the camaraderie and adventure and plain old endorphin-releasing physical exertion that made them carry on with such an unviable occupation. Or was it something else? Something more difficult to describe.

One evening, when Mr M set off on his

daily swim, my daughter and I sat next to a couple of fisherwomen who were perched on the walkway, drying their hair. Pleased to have an all-female audience of four, he proceeded to perform his best butterfly stroke for our benefit, stopping to tread water every so often to wave or roll upside down, waggle his feet and indulge in the kind of husbandly behaviour that ensured our attention did not stray too far from him. Watching him frolic thus, Vijayan's wife grinned and said, 'Your man is no different to ours, you know. Those mad enough to love the sea will find any excuse to keep going back in.'

POSTSCRIPT

ALTHOUGH WE LIVED IN OUR HOUSE ON THE BEACH for over a year, it now lies empty for large periods of time due to the ever-changing circumstances of our lives. Leaving it to languish unoccupied is, in my opinion, a crying shame given the struggle we underwent to build it. Especially those trysts with Trivandrum Corporation.

It is, therefore, on offer to anyone who wishes to occupy it while finishing a written piece of work (novels, non-fiction, screenplays, poetry collections, anything that requires creativity and—that rapidly shrinking resource—imagination). No proof/offer of publication is required because this is a scheme meant to encourage struggling writers. However, occupancy will need to be restricted to six-month periods in order to allow more people to benefit.

Please apply using less than thousand words to explain why you require a place like this to finish your work. A small sample of your writing will also be helpful. This can be sent via email to: www.jaishreemisra.com.

I expect no rent or payment except for a complimentary signed copy of your work when it is published (inshallah). However, you will need to love the place as if it were your own. A maid visits the plot every day to water the plants and clean the compound. She would be happy to help clean the house or do some simple cooking, but such extra tasks will need to be negotiated and paid for directly.

I also apologise in advance for not being able to respond to everyone who applies. If you hear nothing a month after you write to me, please assume you have not been chosen on this occasion.

Warning: The house has been named 'Ocean Spray' for very good reason. The sound of booming surf in the middle of the night is probably unsuitable for anyone with a well-developed amygdala.